IN YOUR FACE

THE CULTURE OF BEAUTY and You

Shari Graydon

Art by **Karen Klassen** *&* **Katy Lemay**

annick press
toronto + new york + vancouver

Revised edition edited by Paula Ayer
Copyedited by Pam Robertson
Proofread by Elizabeth McLean
Designed by Natalie Olsen/Kisscut Design
Cover art by Karen Klassen
First edition edited by Pam Robertson

Annick Press Ltd.

We acknowledge the support of the Canada Council for the Arts, the Ontario Arts Council, and the Government of Canada through the Canada Book Fund (CBF) for our publishing activities.

ONTARIO ARTS COUNCIL
CONSEIL DES ARTS DE L'ONTARIO
50 YEARS OF ONTARIO GOVERNMENT SUPPORT OF THE ARTS
50 ANS DE SOUTIEN DU GOUVERNEMENT DE L'ONTARIO AUX ARTS

Cataloging in Publication
Graydon, Shari, 1958–, author
In your face : the culture of beauty and you / Shari Graydon;
illustrated by Karen Klassen and Katy Lemay.—Revised edition.

Includes bibliographical references and index.
ISBN 978-1-55451-666-7 (pbk.).—ISBN 978-1-55451-667-4 (bound)

1. Beauty culture. 2. Beauty, Personal—Psychological aspects. 3. Feminine beauty (Aesthetics).
I. Lemay, Katy, 1970–, illustrator II. Klassen, Karen, 1977–, illustrator III. Title.

TT957.G73 2014   j391.6   C2014-900516-4

Distributed in Canada by:
Firefly Books Ltd.
50 Staples Avenue, Unit 1
Richmond Hill, ON L4B 0A7

Published in the USA by Annick Press (US) Ltd.
Distributed in the USA by:
Firefly Books (US) Inc.
P.O. Box 1338
Ellicott Station
Buffalo, NY 14205

Printed in China

Visit us at: www.annickpress.com
Visit Shari Graydon at: www.sharigraydon.com
Visit Karen Klassen at: www.karenklassen.com
Visit Katy Lemay at: www.agoodson.com/katy-lemay/

Also available in e-book format. Please visit www.annickpress.com/ebooks.html
for more details. Or scan

CONTENTS

AFTER

eye color inte

skin tone

Letter from the author

BEAUTY *rules.*

And not just in our fantasies.

Do you ever get the impression that people with great looks are much more likely than everyone else to fall into fame and fortune?

Watch your favorite TV show, scan a few magazine covers at the corner store, or check out the singers who make it big: chances are the faces and bodies you're looking at are more attractive than most of the people you see walking down the street or hanging out in the hallways at school.

Every day, in a thousand ways, we're reminded of how much easier the world seems to be for people blessed with the right hair, face, and body parts. You can't help but wonder whether your own life might be just *that much better* if the reflection looking back at you from the mirror every morning were a bit more like the latest swimsuit model or boy-band star.

Yet ideas about what's "beautiful" change all the time. Your closet probably has evidence of the fact that fashion is awfully fickle: what's considered cool and desirable one month can be *so over* the next. And not everyone has the same tastes—not here in North America, and certainly not in other parts of the world. Open up a foreign magazine or history book: you'll see people whose looks may be admired in their own countries, or would have wowed their friends in the past, but wouldn't turn heads in your crowd.

DOES EVERYTHING COME EASIER *TO BEAUTIFUL PEOPLE?*

BUST

WAIST

HIP

Ever ask yourself why? Why then, and not now? Why there, and not here? Why that look, and not this?

Even though the standards of beauty—not to mention the methods for achieving it—have changed radically over time and across cultures, it seems clear that the desire to look hot is hardwired into human nature. Art in an Egyptian tomb from around 2400 BC shows a slave beautifying a nobleman's feet; a thousand years later, Nefertiti, an acknowledged babe of her time, was big into eyeliner; and aspiring hotties of the 21st century can choose from a seemingly endless array of beauty aids.

It's harder than ever these days to avoid thinking about our looks. Advances in technology have made it easier and faster to capture and transmit images of faces and bodies. When your parents were growing up, cameras were heavy, clunky things, film cost money, and photos were usually shared with only a few people. Now cameras on tiny handheld devices can take our pictures anytime, anywhere, and instantly send them to everyone we know. No wonder some people spend as much time worrying about their online "image" as about how they look in person. (Ever untagged yourself from a photo where your smile looked weird, or fixed your hair before video chatting with a friend?)

IDEAS ABOUT WHAT'S *BEAUTIFUL* CHANGE ALL THE TIME.

In Your Face sets out to discover:

 why we're so fascinated by beauty;

 what we've done over the centuries and across cultures to stand out, fit in, and measure up;

 who gets to decide what's hot and what's not; and

 what forces and sources shape our views.

We will examine the beauty lessons we learn in everything from bedtime stories to blockbuster movies and check out the vast and varied definitions of beauty from all over the world. And our exploration of the enduring appeal of the young and the healthy will help to explain some of the wild things people have done in the past —and are doing today—in pursuit of looking good.

We'll compare the beauty standards applied to guys and girls, and shine some light on the power games that have been played in the name of beauty to keep certain people in their place. Along the way, we'll look at the advantages and the disadvantages (yes, there are some!) of being judged a hot property.

In Your Face goes backstage at beauty contests—both the kind that focus on tiaras and prize money and the kind that happen every day in school hallways and bathroom mirrors. We'll also open the vault on the people who get rich by making the rest of us feel insecure, and expose the gap between what we see and what's actually achievable. And we'll look at how new communications technology, social media, and the internet can affect our perceptions of beauty, in both helpful and harmful ways.

Understanding the pitfalls of trying to look our best won't necessarily inspire us to toss out the tweezers or hair products. But putting beauty into perspective can definitely help us to stop feeling so controlled by it. The treatment (if not the cure) includes valuable reality checks and alternative beauty tips—great strategies for wrestling your feelings about image pressure to the ground.

Once UPON a Time

◇◇◇◇◇◇◇◇◇◇◇◇

WHAT WAS IT FOR YOU?

**Your mother's face? A favorite doll?
That magnificent superhero costume
you wore on your fourth Halloween?
Or do you even remember the first
time you noticed that something
or someone was "beautiful"?**

◇◇◇◇◇◇◇◇◇◇◇◇◇◇◇

Probably not. From the moment we're born, we hear many things described as being beautiful. Beauty becomes something we learn about without even trying. And as soon as we are old enough to follow a fairy tale, we really begin to learn about beauty—especially as it relates to people.

WHAT DOES *"BEAUTIFUL"* MEAN TO YOU?

FINDING THE *"Fair"* IN FAIRY TALES

◇◇◇◇◇◇◇◇◇◇◇◇◇◇◇◇◇◇◇◇◇◇◇◇

From Hans Christian Andersen to the Brothers Grimm to Walt Disney, the stories we hear as kids are full of characters who are incredibly good-looking, or incredibly not: Sleeping Beauty, Beauty and the Beast, the Ugly Duckling… Fairy-tale lessons are very familiar to us before we even enter kindergarten. What do they tell us about beauty?

Heroine

SNOW WHITE AND THE SEVEN DWARFS

Snow White, the fairest of them all

SLEEPING BEAUTY

Aurora, a beautiful princess

Cinderella, who is kind, dutiful, and— yep—beautiful

CINDERELLA

BEAUTY AND THE BEAST

Beauty (or Belle, in the Disney movie), who is charming, kind, and generous (oh, and did we mention beautiful?)

Villain(s)	Love interest	When the hero falls in love with the heroine, she is . . .	Beauty "lessons"

Her older (and less beautiful) stepmother, who's so jealous she tries to kill Snow White—twice

A handsome prince

Unconscious

Beauty makes women jealous and crazy; older women are especially jealous of younger women. Beauty is the ticket to being rescued by a good-looking guy and living "happily ever after."

A wicked, ugly fairy, who puts a sleeping curse on her

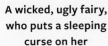

A handsome prince

Unconscious

If you're beautiful, a good-looking, rich guy will fall in love with you and save you, even if you're passed out at the time (who cares if you're cool or fun to hang out with?).

Her ugly, jealous stepsisters and stepmother, who order her around

A handsome prince

Conscious! But decked out in seriously fancy clothes

Beautiful women are good and hardworking, and triumph in the end; unattractive women are mean and vindictive, and have big feet.

In some versions of the story, a handsome but boorish suitor

A handsome prince who has been transformed by a curse into a hideous beast, and can only be changed back by true love

His prisoner

Beauty is only skin deep: a person's character, or inner beauty, is much more important. Those who recognize and choose inner goodness over beautiful exteriors will be rewarded (of course it's the beautiful girl who has to love the ugly guy, and not the other way around).

BEAUTY
AT THE BOX OFFICE

◇◇◇◇◇◇◇◇◇◇◇◇◇◇◇◇◇◇◇

You could consider fairy tales the kindergarten equivalent of beauty school. They teach you the basics. But then you "graduate" to movies for teens and adults, which provide a new level of information (some would say *mis*information) about the power and pitfalls of beauty.

Movies for older audiences may feature less animation, different locations, and more grown-up challenges, but after a while you might start to notice that the character types and basic storylines are very familiar. Fairy-tale lessons resurface in movies time and again. You can probably think of examples that fit the following categories.

PRINCE RESCUES BEAUTIFUL GIRL:

You'd think that *Snow White, Sleeping Beauty,* and *Cinderella* might have exhausted our appetite for this storyline by the time we hit school, but apparently not. Moviemakers are obviously counting on the appeal of a fantasy in which all we have to do is be discovered by our dream date.

PLAIN JANE GETS TRANSFORMED:

At essence, this story suggests that we're all capable of being beautiful if we just work at it. If we buy the right clothes, apply the right makeup, and learn how to walk well, be cool, or fit in, we too can become a beauty queen or catch a good-looking guy.

BEAUTY IS ONLY SKIN DEEP:

The wisdom Belle shows in embracing the Beast, despite his hideous appearance, is echoed in other stories. In the classic play *Cyrano de Bergerac*, for instance, written in 1897, the title character, a witty and romantic poet ashamed of his large nose, hides his love for the beautiful Roxane, and lets the handsome, shallow suitor Christian seduce her using Cyrano's words. Although Roxane is captivated by Christian's hot exterior, what she really falls in love with is Cyrano's beautiful soul, through his writing. The story has inspired dozens of modern adaptations, all delivering the message that true love is more than skin deep.

JEALOUS MUCH?

Even if you've never made your better-looking friend or skinnier stepsister wear rags, scrub floors, or eat poison, feeling envious of another person's beauty is not uncommon.

It's what you do with the envy that makes the difference. Part of the Cinderella story's message is that vindictiveness and spite rank fairly high on the "guaranteed to make you ugly" scale. But imagine if the stepmother and sisters had just fantasized about Cinderella scrubbing the floor, and then gotten a life ...

THE DISNEY PRINCESS LINE SELLS *$3 BILLION* WORTH OF PRODUCTS EVERY YEAR.

PRINCESS POWER

If you're a girl growing up today, chances are the Disney Princesses were your first idea of what a "beautiful woman" looks like. The Disney Princess line, featuring heroines from the company's popular movies, includes more than 25,000 different products, ranging from clothing, toys, and home furnishings to bandages and bike helmets. With $3 billion in sales each year, it's the most popular character franchise in the world, easily outselling even *Star Wars* and *Sesame Street* merchandise.

And what's the image we're buying? Although the princesses vary slightly in skin color (from "white as snow" to "light brown"), they present a uniform ideal of beauty: huge eyes, small noses, heart-shaped faces, flowing hair, and curvy figures with absurdly tiny waists (seriously, where are their internal organs supposed to go?). In the movies, these characters have positive traits in addition to their good looks—for instance, Belle from *Beauty and the Beast* is bright and independent, and Jasmine from *Aladdin* is strong-willed and adventurous—yet the products depict them doing nothing but posing in fancy dresses, looking pretty.

Can you guess the target market for Disney Princess products? Girls aged two to five.

Do you think being surrounded by these images can affect young girls' perceptions of beauty? Or is "princess obsession" harmless make-believe?

GOOD *beauty,* BAD *beauty*

The fairy-tale conventions that equate goodness with beauty and ugliness with evil show up in many contemporary stories. In both animated and live-action movies, one thing you can generally count on is that the heroes and heroines will be better-looking than average. Villains, meanwhile, are often less than physically perfect. How many evil characters can you think of who have a scar, deformity, or disability?

Sometimes, these conventions are reversed: the good guys are ordinary-looking (or at least Hollywood's version of ordinary), and the evil or selfish characters are the conventionally gorgeous ones. (Think of anything involving lovable nerds, cruel jocks, and snarky prom queens.) Maybe movie and TV producers assume we'll find it easier to relate to quirky-looking characters—and to despise ones whose appearances are too flawless. In a way these kinds of portrayals are refreshing, because they send the old "beauty equals goodness" notions out the window. But do they just reinforce another unfair stereotype: that beautiful people are shallow or untrustworthy?

Hollywood HOMELY

You might not know it from fairy tales, but plenty of characters from famous stories are more memorable for their personalities than for their looks. Yet when movie studios produce adaptations of existing books, comics, or plays, they're often tempted to give the characters minor makeovers.

In the novel *Jane Eyre,* for instance, the title character is described as plain (though she's passionate and independent), and her love interest, Mr. Rochester, is heavy browed and harsh featured. Yet the actors who have played these characters in the many movie adaptations are usually far from plain—most of them are downright gorgeous. Similarly, in the *X-Men* comics, the character Wolverine is short and stocky, yet the actor who plays him in the movies—Hugh Jackman—is definitely not.

Even when a character on screen is supposed to be ordinary-looking or unattractive, movie and TV producers' definitions of those concepts usually don't match the rest of the world's. TV shows and movies frequently feature characters who

WHAT KIND OF MESSAGE DOES IT SEND WHEN EVEN THE "UGLY" PEOPLE WE SEE ON SCREEN ARE ACTUALLY *GOOD-LOOKING?*

are referred to as unappealing, average-looking, or unable to get a date. Sometimes the whole plot depends on us seeing them this way. But more often than not, these "homely" characters are played by perfectly cute (or even extremely beautiful) actors, who merely wear glasses, unglamorous clothing and outdated hairstyles, or fat suits to indicate their "ugliness."

What kind of message does it send to the rest of us when even the "ugly" people we see on screen are actually good-looking? When we're watching a movie or TV show where an ordinary guy or girl is constantly referred to as ugly or fat, we might start to wonder if the characters are delusional, or we might even start seeing people in that way, too.

THINGS COULD BE WORSE

So you're in the change room at your favorite clothing store, trying on some jeans. But here's the thing: if the waist fits, the butt's too baggy, or if the pants hug your rear, the waist is too big.

It happens, sure, but it could be worse. At least you're not built like a Disney heroine or video game babe! Take Jasmine from the movie *Aladdin*, or Lara Croft from *Tomb Raider*. If they were suddenly transformed into real women, with the same bodily proportions, they'd have enormous difficulty buying clothes. They'd probably need a size 2 to fit their waists and a size 8 or 10 to fit everything else!

REALITY *CHECK*

In everything from movies and fashion magazines to reality TV shows and even commercials, many stories focus on whether or not a woman's appearance is up to scratch. Female characters tend to suffer much more beauty pressure than males. As a result, we need a whole new category to describe the rare stories that feature a heroine who challenges the idea that her looks are all that's important about her.

Consider Robert Munsch's kid's story *The Paper Bag Princess*. In it, the princess, Elizabeth, outsmarts the dragon who has destroyed her castle and clothes. But when she arrives at the dragon's cave to rescue her abducted prince (and intended future husband), Ronald is so ungrateful that he takes one look at her messy hair and paper bag dress and tells her she stinks.

Elizabeth replies, "Ronald, your clothes are really pretty and your hair is very neat. You look like a real prince, but you are a bum." And she decides not to marry him after all.

A big part of what makes the story funny is that it messes with what readers expect. Unlike many fairy tales, Elizabeth is not your typical damsel in distress, passively waiting to be rescued. Smart and fearless, she defeats the dragon herself. Then she gives Ronald the boot because he's so petty that he can't see past her clothes to appreciate her courage and intelligence.

No doubt about it, Cinderella and Snow White have some romantic appeal. But when you live in the real world without fairy godmothers and miracle-inducing kisses, a little kick-butt attitude goes a long way.

BEAUTY MYTHS, GREEK STYLE

Some of the stories we tell about beauty go back even further than fairy tales. And just like fairy tales, stories from Greek myths keep showing up in current entertainment, and have shaped our attitudes and even our language about looks. Here are three of the most famous ones. What do you think of the "lessons" they deliver?

MYTH

TOO-HOT HELEN

If *People* magazine had been around in Ancient Greece, Helen of Troy would have topped the Most Beautiful People list. Practically every guy in the country wanted to marry her, but Menelaus won her hand and became king. When a handsome dude named Paris stole Helen away to his home in Troy, Menelaus sent a thousand ships to get her back, sparking the Trojan War.

Lessons: Beauty causes *big trouble*. It makes people do daring and crazy things. Beautiful women are prizes to be won. (Does Helen actually *do* anything in this story, besides sitting around being gorgeous while men fight over her? Uh-uh.)

Cultural influence: If someone tells you that your face could "launch a thousand ships," take it as a compliment—they're comparing you to Helen.

MYTH

MIGHTY APHRODITE & ADORABLE ADONIS

Aphrodite was the goddess of beauty and love. She became infatuated with Adonis, the handsomest of men. Unfortunately, when Adonis was out hunting one day, another god, jealous of his looks, sent a wild boar to attack him. Aphrodite, though she wept and pleaded with the Fates, was unable to prevent him from dying.

Lesson: Even the gods can be driven to envy and obsession by someone's good looks.

Cultural influence: Ever heard someone refer to a super-buff guy as "an Adonis?" Here's where it comes from.

MYTH

REVENGE ON NARCISSUS

Narcissus was a heartbreaker, with all sorts of nymphs drooling over his good looks. One day, he knelt by a pool of water to take a drink. When he caught sight of his reflection on the surface, he fell head over heels in love—with himself! The harder he tried to embrace the person he saw in the pool, the more frustrated he became, because all he ever did was make waves that wrecked his image. Eventually he died of a broken heart.

Lesson: Beauty makes some people so vain they can only love themselves.

Cultural influence: Today we use the word "narcissist" to describe a person who is filled with self-admiration and unable to feel anything for anyone else.

DOUBLE
Take

The reason schools don't need to offer Beauty 8 or Good Looks 10 is because you've been learning these lessons—whether they're true or not!—forever.

What's important, though, is to know where the messages are coming from and what they mean. From picture books to movies, from myths to video games, the stories passed down from one generation to another and retold in ever-evolving ways shape our views about beauty—what it is and how it affects people.

In looking past the messages about beauty that just don't work in the real world, are there any *positive* lessons we've learned?

Having enough smarts to slay the dragon yourself lets you make your own choices, as opposed to sitting around and hoping to "be chosen."

It's normal to experience envy; almost everyone feels it at one time or another. Vindictiveness, however, as demonstrated by the evil characters in fairy tales, is a turn-off.

If you're female it's best not to count on being rescued by a prince because:
a) he might not show up, and
b) who's to say you'll want to hang out with him, or go where he wants to take you, if he does?

It's possible to bring out people's inner beauty just by loving them.

Even if you're not an ogre or a beast, inner beauty— warmth, intelligence, generosity, a sense of humor—is a handy thing to have. It can help you attract friends and get what you want in the world.

Self-confidence is good; self-infatuation is not.

The EYE of the Beholder

YOU'RE GUSHING TO YOUR FRIENDS

about your latest crush—maybe the shy basketball player who sits behind you in math, or the actor who plays the brooding vampire on that TV show. "He's just so beautiful," you sigh.

◇◇◇◇◇◇◇◇◇◇◇◇◇

"Are you kidding?" your friends say. *"Him?!"*

Swept away by someone's looks, we often forget how individual our responses to beauty can be. And that's not even taking cultural differences into account. It makes you wonder how some physical characteristics—blond hair, for instance, or height—came to be considered attractive. Who got to decide?

INDEFINITE *Definitions*

Attempts to come up with a way of applying scientific principles to the measurement of beauty have just never panned out—but that hasn't stopped people from trying!

ANCIENT GREECE

The Greeks had elaborate theories about what was beautiful and what wasn't. They even thought you could define the perfect human being as a mathematical formula, applying ideals of symmetry, shape, and proportion.

RENAISSANCE

Artists during the Renaissance argued that the perfect face could be divided equally into thirds: the distance from the hairline to the eyebrows should be the same as the distance from the eyebrows to the lower edge of the nostrils, and from the nostrils to the chin. The space between the eyes was supposed to be equal to the width of the nose. These ideals influenced art for centuries.

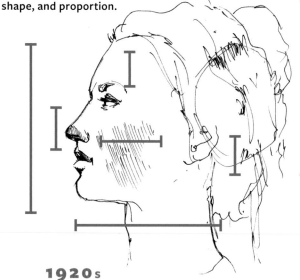

1920s

A judge for one Atlantic City beauty pageant came up with a measurement system to determine the pageant winner in a "scientific" manner. The judge had a great time measuring all the contestants, but the system itself was ultimately tossed out. As another judge commented: "We found you can't judge a woman's beauty piecemeal; you have to take the whole woman at once."

TODAY

Scientists are still working away to quantify why we find certain people more beautiful than others. Every so often, the news media will report on a study claiming to have identified the ideal ratios for facial attractiveness. You can even upload a photo onto a website or use an app to get a number with your "beauty score." But can a formula really measure who's hot and who isn't? According to the "ideal" ratios, both George Clooney and Angelina Jolie would be considered unattractive. Tape measures gauge numbers, but beauty is clearly a bit more mysterious.

From the PAINTERS' PERSPECTIVE

Painters and other artists through the ages have depicted remarkably different ideals of human beauty. Remember Aphrodite, the Greek goddess of beauty and love? In Roman myth she was known as Venus, and she's been vividly imagined by many artists. Each portrayed the woman who was said to embody "beauty" in a different way:

 The *Venus de Milo*, a classic Greek statue from the second century BC, has voluptuous curves and not much of a waist.

 In *The Birth of Venus* by Renaissance painter Sandro Botticelli, the goddess has small breasts, a round tummy, and curly blond hair.

 Both Flemish master Peter Paul Rubens and the 16th-century Italian artist Titian painted Venus as noticeably plump by today's standards.

BOTTICELLIS ON A DIET?

In 2012, an Italian artist named Anna Utopia Giordano digitally altered the bodies of women in famous paintings to fit 21st-century standards of beauty. Using Photoshop, she slimmed down lush hips, stomachs, and thighs and enlarged the breasts of nudes in masterpieces by Titian and Botticelli, among other artists.

The strange sight of size-zero bodies in place of the voluptuous originals is a startling reminder of how cultural ideals of women have changed. Clearly today's "plus-size" dimensions were once celebrated, not criticized. What's considered beautiful and ideal depends—as the saying goes—on the eye of the beholder.

HAIR ADVICE
Through the Ages

◇◇◇◇◇◇◇◇◇◇◇◇◇◇◇◇◇◇

Changes in fashion don't always take centuries. Have you ever opened up one of your parents' high school yearbooks and rolled your eyes at how incredibly geeky everybody looked? Even if the pictures are only head shots, the hairstyles alone are dead giveaways that the pictures were taken decades ago.

The history of hair fashion is a good way to put your own hair woes in perspective and see how beauty standards change over time. Through the centuries, women in particular have ironed and curled, dyed and teased, piled and pinned their hair into a wide variety of shapes and styles.

Medieval times

Shave your hairline to achieve today's hottest look, a long forehead! Don't forget to repeat every day or two to avoid stubble.

17th to 18th centuries

To get that "European aristocrat" vibe, you simply *must* wear a wig. What you'll need: wool to pile the hairdo high, wire to keep it in place, and flour to powder it gray or white (this will make you look young and soft). Finally, don't forget some ornaments to decorate it—for fun, try a small birdcage, live bird optional!

Victorian era

Pile your hair high—
it will make your neck
look longer!

1920s

Short and bobbed is
the mark of modern
sophistication. Think edges
so straight you could use
your hair as a ruler.

1950s

Tease your hair into a
"bouffant"—just like
cotton candy. If your
'do measures more
than a foot across,
you're doing it right.

1960s

Groovy, man! Let your
hair grow long: wear
it straight down your
back or in an afro as a
sign of rebellion.

1980s

Think *big*: perms,
backcombing, and
plenty of hairspray
will help you achieve
maximum volume.

1990s

Do you have naturally
curly or wavy hair? Get
ready to spend hours
every week blow-drying
and flat-ironing it into
submission, because
long and poker-straight
is *the* must-have look.

Just like hairstyles, different body types have gone in and out of style over the ages. Today, thin is undeniably in: 20 years ago, the average fashion model weighed just 8 percent less than the average woman. Today, she weighs *23 percent* less.

In fact, for most of recorded history, the women considered most beautiful have not been so thin that they had to run around in the shower to get wet. Traditionally, plumpness was seen as a sign that a girl or woman had high social status and enough money to ensure she wouldn't starve. Ample curves on a woman were also believed to reflect a good sense of humor and an easygoing nature. As recently as the 1890s, skinny women were considered in North America to be mean-spirited and bad-tempered.

But all sorts of events in the 20th century changed how people thought about beauty, especially in the Western world. And in response to those events, some aspects of physical appearance became more important than others.

THE AVERAGE MODEL WEIGHS *23 PERCENT LESS THAN* THE AVERAGE WOMAN.

WEIGHT DIVISIONS

In most cultures throughout history, being well fed was a sign of wealth, and therefore a good thing. But in modern-day North America, where most of us have easy access to cheap, high-calorie food, obesity has become associated (fairly or not) with lower-income people, who may lack the resources to eat well and exercise regularly.

Meanwhile, people who are better off are usually in a better position to afford things that keep them thin: gym memberships, personal trainers, healthy food, private chefs. Our biases against overweight people, some social critics argue, can be partly blamed on class snobbery.

THOSE BREASTS
Are So Five Years Ago

◇◇◇◇◇◇◇◇◇◇◇◇◇◇◇

Unlike hair, the bodies we're born with are not so easy to change to fit the current style. And yet breasts and butts, for instance, have gone in and out of "fashion" over the years. In some eras, clothes were designed to focus attention on these body parts, and at other times, women were expected to hide or minimize them.

Just for a moment, think about how crazy it is that a body part can ever be declared "unfashionable." Most of us have two thumbs. But imagine if someone decided one day that they were no longer "in," and that it would be better if we disguised them. Clothing designers would create special gloves or complicated sleeves that made thumbs look smaller, or covered them up altogether.

How and why did attitudes change so much over the space of a single century? It helps to know a bit about the way society has historically viewed women, and what they were expected to be and do…

1890s

Throughout the 1800s, the corset was a wardrobe "must" for fashionable North American women: they had to tightly lace the cumbersome undergarments around their torsos to make their waists look smaller, emphasizing their busts and behinds in contrast. This made moving around very difficult, which had the added social benefit of keeping women "in their place"—mostly at home! Additional help on the bust front was available in "falsies" (padding or fake breasts), since voluptuous women with large bosoms were seen to be healthy, modest, and good. The most celebrated beauty of the late 1800s, singer/actor Lillian Russell, was said to weigh close to 200 pounds. In contrast, thinness was sometimes seen to be the mark of an indecent and dangerous woman.

1910S–20S

1950S

In 1908, Parisian designer Paul Poiret created a new, slimmer style of dress and announced, "From now on, the breast will no longer be worn." Easy for him to say! Then World War I gave many women their first opportunity to get jobs, and many Western countries also granted white women the right to vote. Feeling increasingly independent, women abandoned restrictive corsets, giving them enormous freedom to move. But in order to achieve the flat-chested "flapper" look of the 1920s, many women bound their breasts tightly against their rib cages to make their figures look more boyish, along with wearing girdles to minimize their hips. Also, the shorter, often sleeveless dresses made women more self-conscious of their arms and legs, and the suddenly popular slim look gave birth to the 20th century's first dieting craze.

After World War II, women were encouraged to give up their factory jobs to ensure that returning soldiers had work. Governments and retailers in the US and Canada encouraged women to focus on activities considered to be more feminine—like worrying about their looks, and cooking and cleaning! Popular movie stars like Marilyn Monroe and Jane Russell made having curves fashionable again, and doctors suddenly started diagnosing "small breasts" as if it were an illness, and recommending plastic surgery.

1960s

1980s

British fashion model Twiggy became all the rage almost overnight. Her nickname reflected how incredibly thin she was—although 5 feet, 6 inches tall, she reportedly weighed only 91 pounds. The new woman-as-child fashion ideal emerged just as many women were starting to argue for greater equality between men and women. Some social critics believed that fashion was being used to keep women in their place, to focus their attention on dieting to achieve the right body shape—instead of on lobbying to be paid the same wages as men.

Curves made a fashion comeback. Some people credit women's increasing power in the workplace for the change, which was also reflected in dress and blouse styles that included big shoulder pads, designed to help women appear more authoritative at the office. Others point to the fact that cosmetic surgeons were promoting the wider availability of silicone breast implants. Models like Christie Brinkley and Cindy Crawford represented the ideal of the strong All-American Girl.

1990s

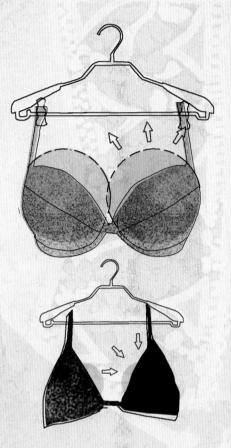

By the following decade, two extremes seemed to be competing for attention. On the one hand, cosmetic surgeons claimed that the pumped-up profiles of popular stars like the surgically enhanced Pamela Anderson were responsible for the continuing trend toward bigger breasts. On the other hand, the waiflike Kate Moss, who was so skinny she sometimes resembled a child, had become the supermodel of the decade. The wasted "heroin chic" look became so popular in the media that health professionals expressed concerns it was promoting dangerous behavior among young women.

2000s

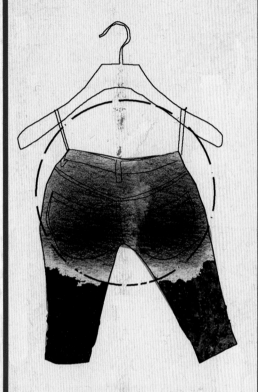

Since the turn of the millennium, the increasingly multiethnic makeup of North American society and entertainment has led to more appreciation of curvier figures, with "bootylicious" icons like Jennifer Lopez and Beyoncé even sparking demand for butt implants and injections. But if curves (natural or not) are in, the ultra-toned look of many models and celebrities proves that fat is still out.

BODY IMAGE *Goes Global*

Our definitions of what's gorgeous and what's not haven't just changed over time; they also vary dramatically from one culture to another. Contrast North American beauty standards with some of the traditional attitudes found in other countries:

 In Brazil, large bottoms and small breasts are seen as desirable assets.

 Native Peruvians, Ugandans, and many Nigerians consider especially full-figured women beautiful.

 Girls in Mauritania, a country in west Africa, are force-fed—up to 16,000 calories a day, enough to feed four male bodybuilders—in order to achieve the ripples of fat and stretch marks that are the height of beauty in their society.

 Some African tribes make deliberate cuts to their skin in order to create scarring, which they view as beautiful.

 In other countries, young people puncture the skin on their face or body with pieces of metal. (Oh, wait a second, those countries include Canada and the United States!)

AROUND THE WORLD, DEFINITIONS OF BEAUTY ARE *EXTREMELY DIVERSE.*

But North American culture is being exported all over the world faster than ever. As a result, the definitions of beauty held up as ideal in TV shows, advertisements, and movies produced here have been imposed on other cultures. Even in some Asian and African countries, where the vast majority of people have dark hair, skin, and eyes, the models celebrated as being the height of beauty are often blond-haired, blue-eyed, and pale-skinned. What's the message to global audiences? North American promotional images and pop culture end up suggesting to millions of people that they are not beautiful the way they are.

Even within North America, definitions of beauty can be tremendously diverse. Both Canada and the United States are made up of people from all over the world whose skin, hair, and eyes reflect a rainbow of colors, and whose body preferences and fashion practices have been shaped by dramatically different cultures. But most of the images in mainstream media show only a very small part of the picture. And underlying that uniformity is a message: if you don't have the right genetic makeup, you will never meet the media's beauty ideals.

MORE TV MORE PROBLEMS

If you had visited the Pacific island nation of Fiji before 1995, you might have been surprised to discover there was no TV, anywhere. What's more, you would have had a hard time finding anyone who had been on a diet, or even heard of an eating disorder.

But in 1998, just three years after TV was introduced, one study found that 15 percent of Fijian girls had tried vomiting to lose weight. And girls who watched TV at least three nights a week were 50 percent more likely to say they were "too fat" than girls who tuned in less often. Did the influence of American TV programs featuring thin stars play a role, or was it just coincidence?

THE RULES
of Attraction

◇◇◇◇◇◇◇◇◇◇◇◇◇◇◇◇◇◇

There are more than seven billion people in the world, and only a couple of dozen of them are supermodels. They're held up as the standard of physical perfection to which we should all aspire, but realistically, most of us won't come close. (Not even the men and women in the media live up to their own images, as we'll see in chapter 9.) And yet every day you can walk down the street and see all kinds of beauty that don't fit the supermodel mold. Ordinary people boasting unfashionably generous thighs or thin lips are attractive for reasons that go beyond the superficials of skin tone and body shape. Their appeal might lie in their unique fashion sense or eyes that light up when they talk.

Increasingly, our ideals are becoming a whole lot more diverse—and more interesting, too. As North American society has grown more multicultural, the once all-white faces held up as beautiful in the media are slowly giving way to a variety of skin colors and ethnicities.

A number of fashion designers and advertisers have featured fuller-figured models —and gotten a lot of attention for it. And some daring trendsetters are even pushing us to accept people of all different ages, shapes, and physical abilities as beautiful, as did the organizers of a 2012 runway show featuring a glamorous 81-year-old model, and a chic British clothing chain that used amputee models in its ads.

DOUBLE
Take

So what does beauty being in the eye of the beholder really mean?
Basically, that it's up to you—and me, and him, and them, and her…
We've all got opinions, and a lot of them clash.

There's simply no predicting. Throughout history and across cultures, people have responded to all sorts of different qualities—both physical and emotional—when checking out one another's looks.

Just as it's impossible for people to agree on the best movie or book of all time, a single definition of beauty doesn't exist.

The images we see in the media reflect only a fraction of the beauty diversity found in the real world.

Tape measures can give you dimensions, but they're useless for judging beauty.

The Young and the HEALTHY

◇◇◇◇◇◇◇◇◇◇◇◇

EVER HEARD THE EXPRESSION

"Age before beauty"? It sums up a common assumption: age and beauty are mutually exclusive. If you're old, then you can't also be beautiful— because youth is an essential ingredient.

◇◇◇◇◇◇◇◇◇◇◇◇◇

This may be difficult to appreciate when you're trying to survive adolescence. But chances are that when adults look at you, they see plump lips, unlined skin, and lustrous hair. With age, these qualities fade: skin wrinkles and hair turns gray or falls out. Advertisers invest a lot of time pointing out how unattractive aging is, and telling older people their lives would be *so* much better if they looked more like you.

DOES BEAUTY
SURVIVE THE
PASSAGE OF TIME?

THE FOUNTAIN *of Youth*

Television, magazine, and web ads for everything from anti-aging creams to Botox to hair dye take as a given that adults would like nothing better than to turn back the clock and recapture their once gorgeous youth. You probably never even register these ads, but for people over 30, the message is inescapable: they're on the downhill slide, and it's not pretty!

From the advertisers' perspective, this is good news: since everybody ages, and most of us buy into the notion that beauty equals youth, there will always be lots of customers for the products they're selling. In fact, worldwide sales of anti-aging products and services top $250 billion a year, and the

market keeps growing. Many women spend hundreds or thousands of dollars per year dyeing their hair to cover gray, injecting Botox in their faces to smooth wrinkles, and buying all manner of youth-promising creams and serums, some costing upwards of $200 for a tiny jar, and often containing some seriously bizarre ingredients (snail slime and human placenta? Check, and check).

Do these products deliver? Most dermatologists agree that over-the-counter creams might temporarily improve the appearance of wrinkles, but can't actually penetrate the skin or "reverse the aging process" as many of them claim.

CREATE YOUR OWN
Anti-Aging Beauty Product!

◇◇◇◇◇◇◇◇◇◇◇◇◇◇◇◇◇◇◇◇◇◇◇◇◇◇

Want a piece of that $250-billion-a-year industry?

The first thing you'll need is a good name for your glorified wrinkle cream.
Just pick one word from each column, and you'll have the next
must-have beauty product to sell to all your friends' moms!

PICK ONE FROM EACH COLUMN:

product name					fights...	active ingredient	
Pro	Repair	Pore	Blasting	Essence	Fine lines	Placenta	Extract
Derma	Care	Wrinkle	Shrinking	Complex	Crow's feet	Algae	Oil
Pharma	Skin	Age	Luminizing	Serum	Dark spots	Emu	Secretion
Nu	Face	Collagen	Perfecting	Booster	Loose jowls	Snail	Acid
Future	Lift	Moisture	Renewing	Concentrate	Droopy eyelids	Pumpkin	Enzyme
Youth	Glow	Time	Rejuvenating	Creme	Mottled patches	Bee	Venom

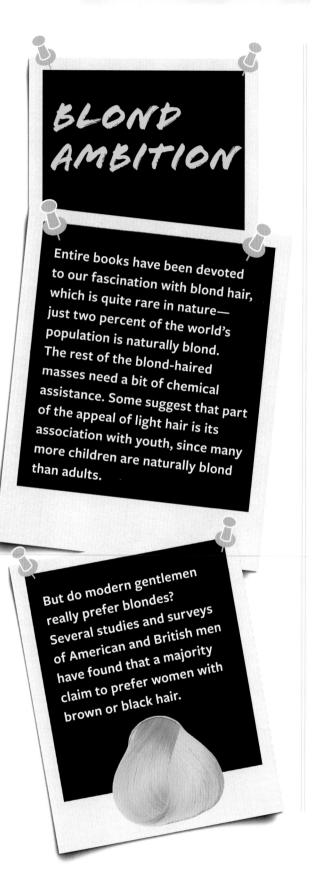

BLOND AMBITION

Entire books have been devoted to our fascination with blond hair, which is quite rare in nature—just two percent of the world's population is naturally blond. The rest of the blond-haired masses need a bit of chemical assistance. Some suggest that part of the appeal of light hair is its association with youth, since many more children are naturally blond than adults.

But do modern gentlemen really prefer blondes? Several studies and surveys of American and British men have found that a majority claim to prefer women with brown or black hair.

How Young IS TOO YOUNG?

◇◇◇◇◇◇◇◇◇◇◇◇◇◇◇◇◇◇◇◇

Fashion has always liked its women youthful—in the 1960s, Twiggy was only 16 when she became the world's most famous style icon.

But in recent years, many of the girls seen on runways and in fashion magazines are so young, it seems elite modeling agents must be scouting for new talent on playgrounds. Most high-fashion female models today start their careers at 13 or 14, and some begin working before they even enter their teens. Strange, but true—many of the models that grown women are encouraged to admire or emulate are literally children, dressed and made up to look like glamorous adults.

Why? Prepubescent models who haven't yet developed breasts or hips are usually easier to fit into the double-zero sizes of

ONE AGENCY
CLAIMED
16-YEAR-OLD
GIRLS WERE
"TOO OLD"
TO MODEL.

most runway fashion. (Which raises the question: why can't they just make the clothes bigger?) And their childlike, innocent look is seen as appealing by many advertising clients and clothing buyers. Modeling agents also claim younger girls are easier to "groom" and control; one agency even said 16-year-old girls were "too old."

Many people have criticized the use of very young models as exploitative. For one thing, models in runway shows have to dress and undress backstage, where there are usually lots of people and cameras around. And very young models, some argue, may not have the maturity to deal with many common aspects of the industry, like being rejected by designers, treated disrespectfully by photographers, or given access to alcohol and drugs.

There are signs the trend may have peaked, however: in 2012 *Vogue* magazine and New York Fashion Week both announced they would no longer use models under 16.

Beauty SURVIVORS

If our cave-dwelling ancestors had been able to place personal ads in their hunt for a mate, the women's ads probably would have read something like this:

Wanted: Intelligent Jock—Fast enough to outrun wild animals, smart enough to outwit them, coordinated enough to hunt them, and strong enough to carry the dead ones home.

The guys' ads would no doubt have been a bit shorter:

Mother Needed: Able to get pregnant, give birth, and feed kids.

The name of the game was survival, and youthfulness and good health were key to ensuring that. As a result, they became essential ingredients in defining a person's attractiveness. Many centuries later, they still are.

One psychologist puts it this way: "Beauty is health. It's a billboard saying, 'I'm healthy and fertile. I can pass on your genes.'"

This theory argues that beauty is not so much in the eye of the beholder as it is in the *circuitry* of the beholder. In other words, some people claim human brains are hardwired to be attracted to young and healthy bodies that appear to be able to help us have children.

of us are no longer hunting wild game for our supper. We don't need to use a cave dweller's criteria when choosing a partner. Our selection process has become much more sophisticated and our attractions to other people are no longer driven solely by biology. We have sex for more reasons than just to have kids.

And yet old patterns are difficult to shake; the way we judge beauty today obviously has its roots in the past.

Take skin, for instance. Even though acne still ranks high on most teens' "things that suck" list, people's skin used to be vulnerable to even worse problems.

Before the days of antibiotic medicines, invented in the 1940s, many infectious diseases, like chicken pox or measles, ravaged people's faces. As a result, those with clear, smooth, and even-toned skin were seen as disease-free—and as a result were more appealing.

In northern cultures of light-skinned people, pale skin became especially prized in part because it allowed you to more easily detect signs of disease. In contrast, darker skin would better conceal evidence of smallpox or jaundice.

But light skin burns very easily, so in especially sunny climates it's an unhealthy disadvantage. Dark skin evolved as protection against the sun, and people living in hotter places developed different beauty rituals to help them identify who was healthy and who wasn't.

The notion of this ideal dates back to Charles Darwin, the 19th-century British naturalist who developed the theory of evolution. He argued that over the course of millions of years, certain physical features and behaviors triumphed because they served a purpose in helping animals or humans to escape the dinosaurs' fate. Other traits and characteristics disappeared because those displaying them weren't selected as often as mates.

Darwin's theory of natural selection has had a lot of influence on how we think about beauty. It suggests that physical attraction is nature's way of ensuring that a species survives.

But we've evolved over the millennia. Most

DECEITFUL LOOKS

Relying on the narrow set of cues that our cave-dwelling ancestors used to judge health, beauty, and the ideal mate would be risky business in North America today. For one thing, we've invented all sorts of ways to fake beauty—from makeup and hair dye to face-lifts and liposuction. Who knows what's real and what's been bought and paid for anymore?

Secondly, North American communities are much larger and more racially diverse than the small groups in which our ancestors lived. Today, features that might have predicted health in one race thousands of years ago—like size or skin tone—have been influenced and altered in combination with those of other races. As a result, they may no longer be reliable indicators of health.

Some scientists argue that even though we consciously realize all these things, parts of our brains haven't caught up to 21st-century reality. They say we're still programmed to respond to the same kinds of cues that got our ancestors excited.

But others say we make decisions every day that override our genes' default mode of ensuring the survival of the most beautiful. And there's evidence of that all around.

BEST *FACE* FORWARD

◇◇◇◇◇◇◇◇◇◇◇◇◇◇◇◇◇◇◇◇

Even though the things likely to affect our skin are less life-threatening now, our attachment to making sure we look blemish-free remains as ingrained as ever.

And the skin care and cosmetics industry capitalizes on our desire to put our best, clearest-skinned face forward.

If you suffer from more than the occasional pimple, acne can have a serious effect on your self-esteem. You might be tempted to buy anything that promises to help: cleansers, exfoliants, cover-up, facials, expensive laser treatments, even prescription medications with scary-sounding side effects.

In infomercials for multi-step skin-care "systems" promising a flawless face, former acne sufferers talk about these products as life-changing miracles that deliver happiness and confidence along with perfect skin. While these promises can be seductive, keep in

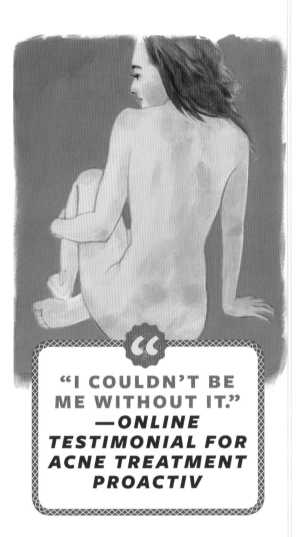

mind that the ads are carefully designed to manipulate (using everything from lighting tricks and makeup to selective editing), and not everyone who uses a product will get the same results. Some acne-fighting "solutions" can be beneficial for certain people (it's best to consult a dermatologist), but others have very little effect. Some can even make matters worse by drying out your skin, causing it to produce more oil and create more pimples.

HEY, NICE SCAR

Maoris and many African tribes practice "scarification"—they deliberately cut themselves and then pour dye, fruit juice, or other irritants into the cuts to inflame them. When the cuts heal, they leave welts. Among many dark-skinned peoples, these permanent welts are seen as beautiful.

In addition, the scars provide evidence that those boasting them are healthy. The idea is that if their bodies were able to withstand the cuts and the irritants and heal effectively, then they must have good immune systems, capable of warding off disease.

In Praise of... AVERAGE?

◇◇◇◇◇◇◇◇◇◇◇◇◇◇◇◇◇◇◇◇◇◇◇◇

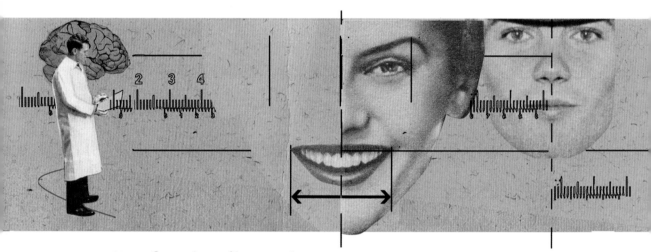

We often describe good-looking people in extreme terms: "He's extraordinarily good-looking" or "She's exceptionally beautiful."

Yet some studies have determined that the faces we find most attractive are actually the ones that are closest to average. When scientists digitally layer images of faces on top of each other to create an "average" composite image, research subjects tend to find the composite face most attractive. Just look at a row of beauty magazines and you'll see evidence of this: many fashion models and actors do have very similar-looking—some might even say interchangeable—faces, and digital photo editing tends to make them look even more alike.

Why is this the case? Science suggests that our brains have an easier time processing features that are closer to average in size and shape, which makes us like them more. According to this theory, a very large nose, or eyes that are spaced really far apart, are more work for our brains to figure out, which makes us like them less. And— Darwin again!—there's also evidence that people with more "average" faces tend to be healthier.

THE
Peacock
SYNDROME

◇◇◇◇◇◇◇◇◇◇◇◇◇◇◇◇◇◇

But wait. . . what about the peacock? There's nothing average about those enormous, extraordinary tail feathers. The thing is, although they may serve to attract peahens, the bigger and showier they are, the harder it is for the male bird to get around. Magnificent tail feathers may make one peacock stand out among others, but they also make it harder for him to survive.

In contrast to the "average = attractive" theory, exaggeration of one particular physical trait—even if the trait doesn't have a built-in health advantage—is also often seen as being beautiful in human beings, too. Very large eyes, for instance, don't necessarily see better, but we tend to find them attractive.

People who are less average-looking can also be more interesting to look at. For all the cookie-cutter beauty we see in mainstream magazines, some of the most memorable and recognizable models have unusual features: a square jaw, a big mouth, or wide-set eyes. Designers and fashion editors often seek out these unconventional beauties, believing their unique looks will set them apart from the rest.

NeW CRITeRIa

In North America today, we may actually pay *less* attention to visual health cues than we used to. In a 2013 study that asked single men and women for their "must haves" in a relationship, the qualities that topped the list weren't looks or health, but trustworthiness and respectfulness. For women, physical attractiveness didn't even make the top five. And though both genders admitted to judging physical qualities that indicated good health and hygiene—like having clean, healthy-looking teeth—most were more likely to be turned off by a potential date's bad grammar than by bad hair or unfashionable clothes.

Speed-dating studies have found that even when people say beforehand that they want to date someone attractive, when they actually meet potential partners face to face, their criteria change. (Maybe they find the pretty girl boring, and a less model-worthy one fun and interesting.)

DOUBLE
Take

So do our judgments about what's hot come hardwired into our brains?
Or have we managed to short-circuit them over time? Probably some of both.

Here's what we *do* know:

If you were born healthy, you already have an advantage in the beauty stakes.

Contrary to the publicity it gets, "average" may actually be more attractive than it sounds.

Unlike some species, we humans adapted instead of dying off. In the process, we opened up all sorts of different ways to value people.

Don't knock the benefits of youth. It may not feel like a powerful beauty weapon, but it is.

The mysteries of attraction can't be explained by biology alone.

SUFFERING
Is
Optional

◇◇◇◇◇◇◇◇◇◇◇◇◇◇

THERE'S AN OLD FRENCH SAYING:
You have to suffer to be beautiful.
**And anyone who's ever spent 10 hours walking
around in four-inch heels or woken up
the day after a tough weight-training session
would probably agree.**

◇◇◇◇◇◇◇◇◇◇◇◇◇◇◇

Through the ages and all around the world, human beings seem to have come up with an unlimited number of ways of inflicting pain on ourselves in pursuit of looking good. Some are so bizarre it's hard to believe anybody would actually engage in them. But other—sometimes equally strange—practices are so familiar to us we don't even think about them.

The question is, why?

?

WHY ARE WE
WILLING *TO SUFFER*
FOR THE SAKE OF
LOOKING GOOD?

ALL *Decked Out*

✧✧✧✧✧✧✧✧✧✧✧✧✧✧✧✧✧

Although we might think of makeup, piercings, and tattoos as recent trends, they've actually been around forever.

The traditional theory is that we enhance our bodies, faces, and hair with jewelry, ink, paint, and clothing for the same reasons birds display colorful plumage: to attract a little attention, and (on a conscious level or not) to find a mate. But is it really as simple as that?

Some feminine beauty practices seem to be all about pointing out not just that "we're beautiful," but that "we're better." For centuries, a key way to do this was to flash your status by drawing attention to the fact that you were so wealthy you didn't have to work. The strategies varied in terms of how much pain they involved, but ranged from skin-whitening and corset-wearing in Europe and North America to foot-binding

in China. In one way or another, the effects of such practices proclaimed: "I live a pampered life." Consider: people with crunched toes require servants to carry them around; Caucasians who were able to avoid working in the fields maintained pale complexions; and those wearing restrictive clothing were unable to do physical labor.

These days, the relationship between beauty practices and social class is less simple. Grooming routines that used to signal free time and money have become accessible to many more people. Still, certain style and adornment choices may indicate things to us about the wearer's social standing and education: we might make assumptions about a man covered in tattoos, or a woman with dyed blond hair and sky-high heels. Most of us make judgments based on such details all the time, probably without even realizing it. And at least some of the time, we're way off the mark.

FROM *Princess* TO *Waitress:*
THE LIFE OF A BEAUTY TREND

 1 Wealthy women adopt some impractical beauty practice. Say, long, painted fingernails, which get damaged or in the way when you're doing any kind of work with your hands.

 2 The trend filters down to less affluent women, who want to emulate the look. As painted nails become more popular, more nail salons start popping up and manicures become cheaper due to competition.

 3 As more and more women start adopting the look—sometimes taking it to an extreme—it becomes less desirable to the wealthy trendsetters. Some might dismiss long, elaborately painted fingernails as tacky. Of course, it's very much an eye-of-the-beholder thing: one person's "glamorous and fun" rhinestone-and-glitter manicure is another person's "vulgar nightmare."

MANUAL LABOR?

Nail polish was once reserved for royalty: in ancient China, lower-class women caught with decorated digits could be sentenced to death! Traditional methods of coloring nails included henna, gold, flower petals, and blood. Then in the 1920s a Frenchwoman invented modern nail polish by tinkering with the formula for car paint. Soon after, the introduction of Technicolor let movie stars show off vibrant red manicures, and the painted-nail trend took off.

INDEPENDENCE *Day*

◇◇◇◇◇◇◇◇◇◇◇◇◇◇◇◇◇◇◇◇◇◇

Other beauty behaviors evolved as a means of marking the passage from childhood into adulthood.

For some African tribes, certain scars are created specifically to show that a young man or woman has passed from one stage to another. One theory is that pain is a necessary ingredient of the ritual: living through it demonstrates that the person is mature enough to handle the challenges that face adults.

Of course, not all beauty rituals involve pain. But in North America today, some experts think that kids' interest in dyeing their hair, piercing their body parts, or experimenting with other fashion choices is evidence of an ingrained impulse for rites of passage. They argue that because our culture doesn't provide such rituals, young people have to make up their own.

Sometimes fashion and adornment choices simply allow you to assert your individuality, or to proclaim a separate identity from your parents: a nose piercing, a skull tattoo, or heavy black eyeliner can be a very effective way of saying "I'm not your little girl anymore."

SUN OR SHADE

You may have heard the story about how suntans came to be popular: before the 1920s, in Western countries, fair skin was prized. But then in 1923, the influential French fashion designer Coco Chanel came home from vacation with a suntan (which she reportedly got by accident!). Suddenly a golden-brown glow became the look to covet. In contrast to earlier times, a dark tan came to be seen as a mark of free time, not evidence of hard work outdoors. The message it sent: "I just spent two weeks drinking piña coladas on a tropical beach."

Since then, vacations to sunny places have become more affordable, and the pale-skinned among us have invented ways to get brown without going anywhere near a beach: tanning salons, sprays, bronzers, and creams. But now that we know about the skin cancer risks that come from spending hours in a tanning bed, or on the beach coated with baby oil, a deep tan is no longer a desirable look for many people. Still, the tanning business brings in $5 billion a year in the US—that's a lot of people willing to risk a potentially fatal illness for a sun-kissed appearance.

MAKING UP

People have been slapping natural and unnatural substances on their faces for all of recorded time.

Today, our cosmetics options are nearly limitless: visit a drugstore or makeup retailer and you'll find products to address all sorts of "problems" that you might not have known existed—everything from shiny eyelids to rough cuticles. Spend too much time immersed in the beauty hype and you might start to wonder if there's *any* condition or feature that's not in need of improvement!

Still, we usually don't think of cosmetics as causing suffering (unless it's to your bank account). But in fact, the ingredients that go into our makeup, soaps, shampoos, and lotions are not always pretty. A recent Canadian study revealed 10,500 different industrial chemicals used as ingredients in personal care products. The worst 12—ingredients linked to cancer, reproductive problems, severe allergies, asthma, and other health concerns—were found in nearly 80 percent of products. What's more, many products don't even list ingredients on the label, or they fess up to generic ingredients like "fragrance" that can include hundreds of unidentified, possibly harmful chemicals. And in both Canada and the US, what goes in our soap, lotions, and cosmetics doesn't have to undergo health studies before the products end up on the shelves.

But nobody's forcing us to eat makeup and lotions, right? So why should we worry about chemicals? Well, ingredients in cosmetics can be absorbed through the skin, inhaled (if we're talking powders and sprays), and—in the case of lipsticks and balms—even ingested. They can also cause problems in the environment long after we rinse them down the drain.

Some of the time, these toxic substances are found in small amounts—maybe too small to have any effects. But many scientists and environmental activists say there's cause for concern, and that we should look more closely into what goes into our cosmetics before slathering them all over our faces and bodies.

#

THE AVERAGE PERSON USES 9 DIFFERENT PERSONAL CARE PRODUCTS A DAY, CONTAINING *126 DIFFERENT INGREDIENTS*.

Death Becomes Her?!

◇◇◇◇◇◇◇◇◇◇◇◇◇◇◇◇◇◇◇◇◇◇

Even the strangest cosmetic concoctions for sale today seem incredibly safe compared to what people used in the past:

Middle Ages

In pursuit of a pale complexion, women attached leeches—as in little slimy bloodsuckers found in lakes— to their faces. This drained the color from their cheeks (loss of blood tends to have that effect) and often caused them to pass out.

Renaissance

Women achieved pale skin by applying lead mixed with egg white, lemon juice, or vinegar. You've heard of lead poisoning? Unfortunately, they hadn't. They experienced it instead, in the form of stomach pains, vomiting, comas, and sometimes even death.

18th century

When rosy cheeks came back into fashion, rouge made from sulfur and mercury was used— until it became clear that the concoction was causing inflamed gums and tooth loss.

1930s

Coal tar employed in early eyeliner and mascara sometimes resulted in blindness.

BRING ON
the
Needles

◇◇◇◇◇◇◇◇◇◇◇◇

Even though you don't see a lot of senior citizens with multiple piercings or visible tattoos, the practices have been around for centuries.

But until recently, tattoos had a reputation as the decoration of choice for sailors, truck drivers, and bikers. They were seen as a mark of their wearer's ability to withstand pain like a "real" man. They certainly didn't appeal to teenage girls, and you couldn't get one at the mall. As for piercing, it used to be confined almost entirely to earlobes.

Now that both have become much more mainstream in North America, the question is often not if, but what and where? On the tattoo front, the options range from a discreet horoscope sign on your lower back to the in-your-face approach that sees your forearm double as a scene from a martial arts movie.

Piercings have gradually expanded their territory, too. People seeking to make

an edgy fashion statement might go for tongue studs, eyebrow or cheek rings, or piercings through just about any other body part you can think of.

And the beauty impact? It definitely comes down to an eye-of-the-beholder thing. One person's enhancement is another's radical disfigurement. You might turn off as many people as you turn on!

Maybe that's part of the appeal. Getting some needlework done isn't quite as difficult as the maturation rituals you might go through in a tribal culture, but it's not without risk. Some piercings are particularly tricky: tongue studs, for instance, can damage teeth or cause persistent infections. Safety issues also come into play anytime needles are involved. Then there's the "what was I thinking" factor: 5 or 10 years down the road, will you want to make a different beauty statement? Tattoo removal is a hugely growing business, and the removal process is often more painful than getting the tattoo in the first place.

A HANDY GUIDE TO
Hair Removal

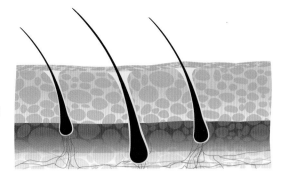

Ancient Sumerians used tweezers to remove hair, Arabians used string, and Egyptians used beeswax and a mixture of starch, arsenic, and calcium oxide.

There's even evidence that Paleolithic man shaved with sharp rocks and seashells. Pity, too, the poor girls of the Elizabethan age: their mothers applied bandages soaked in vinegar and cat dung to their hairlines in order to get those high foreheads mentioned earlier. Regardless of which hair-removal method we're talking about, you can be sure that wincing and grimacing were involved.

Hair-removal technology has come a long way in the past 20,000 years. Unfortunately, given the tendency of hair to grow back, if your goal is the smooth-skinned look, you'll still have to use one of these methods regularly.

HAIR-REMOVAL METHODS:

	1 Shaving	**2** Waxing	**3** Epilation	**4** Depilatory creams	**5** Electrolysis	**6** Laser hair removal
THE PITCH	Use a super-sharp blade to cut off visible hair (careful around the corners!)	Pour hot wax on your skin and tear out your hair by the roots	Use an electrical device (basically a set of rotating tweezers) to rip out hair	Smear your skin with a chemical cream that dissolves hair on contact	Insert a needle into each individual hair follicle to electrocute the root	Zap hair away with a laser beam
PROS	Quick, easy, inexpensive	Hair-free skin for weeks	Long-lasting results	Fast, easy, painless (if used as directed)	Permanent	Reduces hair significantly
CONS	Scratchy stubble may return within approximately 20 minutes	How painful do you think this sounds? Take that, and multiply by 100	Yes, you are correct: this DOES sound like a form of torture	Smells terrible, can burn or blister skin	How much free time do you have? You're going to need it	Say goodbye to your college fund

CELEBRITY ARMPIT HAIR SHOCKER!

Dressed in a designer evening gown for the premiere of her new movie in 1999, actor Julia Roberts raised her arm to wave to the assembled crowd. The cameras clicked furiously, and the next day the scandalous photograph was reprinted in newspapers all over the world.

Ms. Roberts had committed one of the most serious beauty crimes possible—in North America, at least: she had failed to shave her armpits. "You'd think it was a chinchilla that I had under there, the way the world responded," she said to a friend. But Ms. Roberts was obviously more interested in her then-boyfriend's response than the world's: like many Europeans, actor Benjamin Bratt reportedly preferred the natural look.

Since then, famous women including Lily Allen, Drew Barrymore, and Beyoncé have had long-lens cameras zoom in on their armpit stubble, to similarly appalled media reaction. Lady Gaga even made a fashion statement with thatches of (fake) blue underarm hair. Who knows—maybe these glamorous celebrities will start a trend for creatively styled pits?

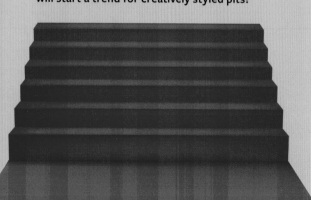

His AND Hers HAIR

In the 1970s, actor Burt Reynolds, the first male "centerfold" to pose nude in a woman's magazine, was covered in body hair. And women were wild about him. Contrast that with today, when most of the guys flogging cologne or underwear in glossy magazines appear to be completely hair-free.

Body hair removal for men isn't a totally new thing—there's evidence that men in ancient Egypt and India preferred the smooth look. But in North America, before the 1990s, the idea of a man waxing away his chest hair, shaving his legs, or even discreetly "manscaping" with trimmers would have seemed ridiculous, even unmanly, to most people. Hairy chests have made a bit of a comeback among actors and male models, but many guys still feel pressure to look like those bare-chested cologne ads.

Still, women seem to have a much narrower range of acceptable options when it comes to hairiness. In many cultures, body hair and facial hair are seen as masculine, and women who don't get rid of it are often considered "unfeminine." For girls, body hair can even affect their social life—many girls won't go swimming or on a date if they haven't shaved. And thanks to the Brazilian bikini-waxing trend, some young women are convinced they have to remove *all* hair from the neck down, or risk being rejected by guys.

Personal hair preferences vary widely— plenty of people find a little (or even a lot) of body hair sexy. Of course, people may choose to wax or shave just because they like the feeling. But when girls—and some-times guys—are afraid of being ridiculed or called disgusting if they show the tiniest bit of body hair, is their choice really a free one?

Can you imagine if girls had the same hair options guys do? When men don't shave their faces for a day or two, we think they look relaxed and casual, maybe even hot. What if it were no big deal for girls to rock a little leg stubble on the weekend? Or grow out our underarm hair for a new look, the way guys might try out a mustache? Think of the time we'd save, the products we wouldn't have to buy, the (ahem) atten-tion we might get!

BEAUTY BULLIES GET SCHOOLED

In 2012, a man at an airport spotted a young woman who had obvious facial hair. He snapped a picture and uploaded it to the website Reddit with a disparaging comment, and other users piled on, making jokes about the woman's appearance.

Typical depressing story of internet bullying, right? Well, the woman in the photo, Balpreet Kaur, found out what happened, and posted her own comment on Reddit. Rather than reacting with anger or embarrassment, she thoughtfully and generously explained that her Sikh faith forbids her to remove her hair or alter her body in any way.

"By transcending societal views of beauty," she wrote, "I believe that I can focus more on my actions." Her post prompted an outpouring of supportive responses, the original poster apologized, and the story went viral, with Kaur gaining respect and praise for sticking to her beliefs despite powerful beauty pressures.

BREATHLESS
Beauties

◇◇◇◇◇◇◇◇◇◇◇◇◇◇◇◇◇◇◇

Have you heard stories about celebrities having ribs removed to make their waists look narrower?

It's an urban myth that's been told over the years about Cher, Tori Spelling, and Britney Spears, among others—but it's just not true.

Rib removal is highly risky and rarely done, and few reputable plastic surgeons will perform it for cosmetic reasons. Maybe the rumors persist because of the other painful rituals women have undergone in pursuit of a desirable hourglass silhouette. For hundreds of years, women wore tight, uncomfortable corsets to trim their figures. In 16th-century France, ladies-in-waiting were expected to cinch their waists to a maximum of 13 inches around.

Since the late 1980s, pop stars have periodically made style statements by wearing corsets (usually as outerwear, not underwear), and some top fashion designers have showcased them in their collections. Fortunately, for anybody who likes to eat, the punishing undergarment has never really made a mainstream comeback.

Corsets might sound extreme, but women today squeeze themselves into push-up bras, control-top tights, and "body-shaping" undergarments that can be nearly as constricting. Is feeling like a stuffed sausage all day just the price to pay for looking good?

87 PERCENT OF WOMEN IN THE US HAVE EXPERIENCED FOOT PROBLEMS FROM WEARING ILL-FITTING SHOES.

IF THE *Shoe Fits...*

Depending who you ask, women's shoes may be the most torturous beauty custom of our day. Whether your budget accommodates high-end designer shoes or bargain knock-offs, high heels come in everything from four-inch stilettos and modest kitten heels to chunky wedges and platforms. And although they lack the comfort of a pair of sneakers, plenty of women are happy to experience a little discomfort in exchange for the perceived benefits. High heels, in addition to offering greater height and making legs look longer and more toned, also alter a person's posture. Bodies not designed to be strapped into mini-stilts adapt by thrusting out the butt and chest in search of balance, making "assets" look higher and perkier. Is it any wonder some girls think wearing heels will get them extra attention?

Unfortunately, wearing high heels regularly can have major drawbacks. These may include hammertoes, permanently contracted muscles and tendons, nerve damage, and, occasionally, bone fracture. Ouch!

But for lots of young women, the risks seem too far down the road to worry about. Fashion magazines and TV shows have made high heels so desirable that even people who have already damaged their feet are willing to take further risks in order to continue wearing them. A growing number of American women are turning to surgery—not to correct the problems caused by heels, but to have the bones in their feet shaved or shortened, fat injected into their soles for extra cushioning, or even their pinky toes completely removed. All so they can get back into the punishing shoes.

UNDER
the Knife

◇◇◇◇◇◇◇◇◇◇◇◇◇◇◇◇◇◇

From street fights in the 16th century to reality TV stars today, plastic surgery has come a long way.

It was first invented to patch up the faces of young Italian men who used knives instead of fists to resolve their drunken differences on Saturday nights. A few hundred years later, in the late 1800s, the sexually transmittable disease syphilis began eating away at its victims' noses. Plastic surgery was often sought to correct the damage.

But it wasn't until the 20th century, as surgery and anesthetic techniques became more sophisticated, that it became common. During World War II, soldiers were coming back from the European front with their faces so damaged that they were unrecognizable. Surgeons, in addition to trying to save their lives, did everything they could to patch up their faces. Newspaper headlines often characterized the results as nothing short of "miraculous."

The result? Healthy people began considering cosmetic surgery as a possible means of looking more attractive, a perspective encouraged by many of the surgeons themselves. And it's become a widespread

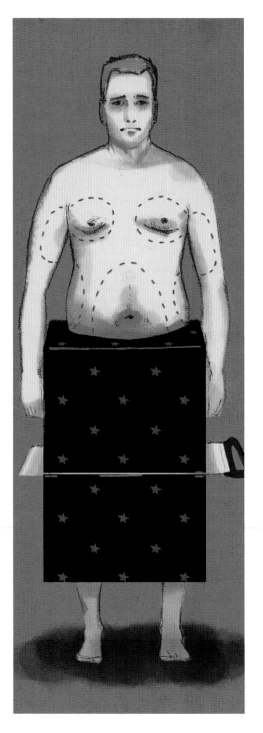

beauty practice—these days Americans undergo nearly 14 million cosmetic procedures annually.

A HANDY GUIDE TO
COSMETIC PROCEDURES

◇◇◇◇◇◇◇◇◇◇◇◇◇◇◇◇◇◇◇◇◇◇◇◇

BOTOX

What is it? Minuscule quantities of the deadly botulinum toxin "A" are injected into your face

Pros Makes wrinkles (and most signs of emotion) disappear

Risks Headaches, bruising, drooping eyelids, inability to smile

FILLERS

What is it? A needle full of cow fat, or chemical "filler," is injected into your face

Pros Temporarily plumps up lips and skin for that youthful, bee-stung look

Risks Allergies, bruising, swelling

BREAST IMPLANTS

What is it? Bags filled with saline or silicone are inserted into your chest

Pros Get the cleavage that nature so cruelly denied you

Risks Rupture, scarring, infection, pain, tissue hardening

BUTT AUGMENTATION

What is it? Silicone or fat from other parts of your body is injected into your bum, or implants are inserted

Pros You'll fill out your jeans better, and boost your chances of getting cast as a music-video extra

Risks Implant shifting, nerve damage, infection, occasionally death

LIPOSUCTION

What is it? Fat tissue from beneath your skin is vacuumed out

Pros Gets rid of fat overnight—dieting and exercise are for suckers!

Risks Lumpy skin, blood clots, punctured organs, occasionally death

TOO MUCH OF A GOOD THING

"Bigger is better" is the message we often hear when it comes to breasts, but for the women carrying them around, they can be a pain in the neck—literally. Especially large breasts can cause chronic neck and back pain, make any kind of athletic activity challenging, and turn clothes shopping into a frustrating experience. Breast reduction surgery doesn't have the same headline appeal as implants, but for many women, young and old, it can bring great relief.

At the opposite end of the spectrum, there are advantages to being an A-cup: for instance, a wide range of clothing choices, and less sagging as you age. And as with many things on the beauty front, the range of what people find attractive is much wider than the media might lead you to believe: lots of guys and girls actually prefer small breasts.

ALL I WANT FOR GRAD IS MY TWO FRONT... *Boobs?!*

Once considered a fairly radical procedure designed primarily for women who had lost a breast to cancer, breast implant operations in the US increased tenfold between 1992 and 2012, from 32,607 to 330,631. It's now the most popular cosmetic surgical procedure, and brand-new boobs have even become the graduation gift of choice for some girls.

Most women who choose to have surgery say they don't want to look like bikini models, they just want to look "normal." The trouble is, when so many women are getting implants, buying push-up "miracle" bras, or being graphically enhanced in photos, it's impossible to know what "normal" is anymore.

The safety of breast implants continues to be hotly debated by doctors, patients, and implant manufacturers. Many women experience extreme pain, hardening of tissues around the implants, or other complications. Often the implants need to be removed or replaced, which can cost as much as the original procedure. Leaks from silicone implants have been linked to health problems, and there's evidence that women

BREAST IMPLANTS DON'T LAST FOREVER: ABOUT *1 IN 4 WOMEN* NEED THEM REMOVED OR REPLACED *WITHIN 5 YEARS.*

Buyer Beware

Next time you run out of horror stories for a sleepover with your friends, try typing the words "plastic surgery" and "botched" into your favorite search engine and see what comes up. You can't believe everything on the internet—and images can be doctored or misleading—but you'll probably find enough to give you second thoughts about having a face-lift or a boob job.

In contrast, the many websites promoting plastic surgery and breast implants tend to downplay the risks of procedures (of course, the site's owners *do* stand to get wealthy if you believe their promises). And while "plastic surgeries gone wrong" are a staple of tabloids and gossip sites, some of the stories you see on TV or in fashion magazines might make such surgeries out to be no big deal. Why? Well, some entertainment media rely on the information provided to them by plastic surgeons, who benefit by emphasizing only the good-news stories.

Keep in mind, too, that for the most part, people who get plastic surgery don't want everyone to know they've had it done. So when a procedure leads to problems or threatens their health, they're sometimes too ashamed or embarrassed to complain—especially if they've paid a whack of money for it.

with implants have a higher risk of dying of breast cancer, since the foreign bodies in their chests can make detection more difficult.

The US Food and Drug Administration only approves saline implants for women 18 years and older, and silicone implants for women 22 and older, recognizing that adolescent bodies are essentially still "works in progress." Breasts can take years to fully develop, and keep changing even in adulthood.

BULKING UP

◇◇◇◇◇◇◇◇◇◇◇◇◇◇◇◇◇

Are you starting to get the impression that it's mostly women and girls who seriously endanger their health for beauty reasons?

Not so fast… These days, more and more guys are engaging in equally risky behavior in the hopes of being seen as more desirable.

Long before Arnold Schwarzenegger made the Terminator a household name, the masculine ideal tended to be athletic and "built." Short guys wishing they were taller are sometimes inclined to build their upper body muscles. And many tall teens who experience beanpole growth spurts that give them height but not weight believe their looks would be improved by adding some bulk. Working out at the gym can help, but it's often a long, slow process. Some turn to protein shakes and other dietary supplements in an effort to counter their scrawniness and get bigger, faster. And the incentives to use these products go beyond looking good.

In competitive sports—from boxing and baseball to track and field—the rewards for winning are often enormous. What athlete wouldn't like to be the first draft pick, or earn an Olympic medal?

Other guys go one step further and use anabolic steroids, which are drugs made from high doses of the male hormone testosterone. Many of these drugs have proven to be effective, and with a weight-training program, they can make a difference to an athlete's size, strength, and speed.

The problem is, in addition to being illegal in sports, anabolic steroids deliver a lot more than muscles. The bulkier physique can be accompanied by a range of side effects, including baldness, breast development, severe acne, stunted growth, kidney damage, heart attack, liver cancer, and shortened life expectancy.

Ironically, it doesn't sound like the average steroid user is likely to improve his chances in the beauty contest of life.

> %
> **A STUDY IN THE US FOUND _5 PERCENT_ OF STUDENTS IN MIDDLE AND HIGH SCHOOL HAVE TAKEN ANABOLIC STEROIDS.**

ROID RAGE

Steroid users aren't usually looking for a personality makeover, but the drugs can sometimes wreak as much emotional damage as they do physical. Extreme mood swings are common, and guys can experience "roid rage," which makes them act violently even though they would never behave that way without the steroids. ("Roid rage" has actually been linked to several murders.)

DOUBLE
Take

Short-term pain for long-term gain can be considered a good deal when it comes to beauty. Getting an ear pierced, for instance, hurts for all of two seconds, and gives you the opportunity to creatively decorate your earlobe for the rest of your life.

But short-term gain for long-term health risks is another matter entirely. Nobody wants an indulgence of vanity today to translate into ongoing suffering 10 or 20 years from now. The trick is in figuring out which fashion choices or procedures are likely to have health or comfort consequences down the road.

There's no simple way of predicting. But here are a few questions you might consider when weighing the pros and cons of future "self-improvement projects." Whether you're contemplating anti-cellulite cream, hair dye, protein supplements, surgery, or a tattoo, ask yourself:

Are there sources of information about this treatment that are independent and trustworthy?

Is the evidence of the procedure's safety based on just a few examples, or have independent experts conducted long-term studies?

How long has this particular process been around? How do people who had it done 10 or 20 years ago feel about it now? If it's still at an experimental stage, how do I feel about being a guinea pig?

Are the impacts of this procedure temporary or permanent?

If they're permanent, can I see myself being happy with this fashion statement 25 years from now?

Is it really safe? Who says so, and do they make money if I believe them?

What risks are involved, and are they worth it?

Is it possible that the treatment or procedure will actually make me look worse?

Am I making this change for my own reasons, or trying to please someone else?

Are my expectations for how this change will affect my life realistic? Am I hoping that a cosmetic process will also alter my personality or make me more popular overnight?

Double
STANDARD

◇◇◇◇◇◇◇◇◇◇◇◇

CLOCK THE TIME SPENT BY

the average 15-year-old guy getting ready to head out the door in the morning, and it might be all of 10 minutes: shower, apply a bit of hair gel, climb into jeans and a T-shirt, and he's done.

◇◇◇◇◇◇◇◇◇◇◇◇◇◇◇◇

Then measure that against the time a typical 15-year-old girl might spend. On top of the shower, she's likely to blow-dry and/or straighten her hair, apply makeup, and ponder each component of her wardrobe. Even if she ends up wearing jeans and a T-shirt, it's likely she'll more carefully consider *which* jeans, and *which* T-shirt.

Why is that, exactly?

Some people chalk it up to female vanity; they claim women are biologically programmed to spend a lot more time gazing at themselves in the mirror.

But read on: the truth is quite a bit more complicated than that.

"MEN ARE MUCH FREER...
WHEN THEY GET A PIMPLE
IT'S LIKE, 'YEAH, I HAVE A
PIMPLE, DEAL WITH IT.'"
—ACTOR DREW BARRYMORE

WOMEN'S WORK?

"Dandyism" and the ancient Greeks aside, when it comes to beautification rituals, by and large our society agrees: it's women's work.

Cosmetics ads, fashion magazines, and beauty blogs consistently deliver the message that women could all be more beautiful with a bit of effort. And much of what we see or read in the media takes it for granted that working hard to look good is just what women *do*: they put on makeup, they fuss over their hair, they wear fashionable clothes, and they worry about being the right size and shape.

Wearing certain clothes, makeup, or hairstyles may well improve your appearance. But saying so also serves the interests of the companies behind such media messages: if people believe them, they're likely to buy more products and magazines, or click on more advertiser-sponsored links.

The "FAIR SEX"

Check out all the words we have to describe attractive human beings and you'll notice that many of them are rarely applied to men. Guys can be cute or handsome, but try calling them lovely, pretty, graceful, exquisite, delicate, stunning, or ravishing.

You might think that women and girls have always been considered the "fairer" sex. Yet you'd be wrong. Throughout history, some cultures have actually revered male beauty above that of women. And rich guys and noblemen in the past typically lavished a lot of attention on their appearance, being able to afford luxurious fabrics and good tailors.

But look around you: it's been more or less downhill for guys on the fancy fashion front for more than a century. In contrast to women's clothing, most menswear today tends to downplay the male physique and help guys melt into the background, wearing the expected business suit, chinos, or jeans, depending on who they are and what they do.

"THERE ARE NO UGLY WOMEN, ONLY LAZY ONES."
—HELENA RUBINSTEIN, COSMETICS MAGNATE

A SHORT HISTORY OF
Male Beauty

1

The early Greeks paid special attention to the male form, believing men to be more beautiful than women. As a result, their art celebrated the ideal male physique and the Olympics were established in part as a tribute to the athletic feats that men were capable of performing.

2

In the 18th century, "dandyism" flourished. Fashionable young British and European men went overboard, wearing decorated velvet jackets, fine silk stockings with frilly garters, corsets, jeweled shoes, and ornate gloves, not to mention calf, thigh, and crotch padding (I'm not making this up).

3

Later in the 18th century, as manufacturing and transportation technology developed, people became very focused on productivity, and it was thought that men's appearances should show them to be serious and effective at work, as opposed to beautiful and elegant. Dark-colored suits became a sort of "uniform" and, compared to women's wear, they haven't changed a whole lot since.

Here's Looking
AT YOU

Try this experiment: flip through a women's fashion magazine and check out the advertisements or fashion spreads. Chances are most of them will feature women. Stop for a moment and try to imagine the photographer taking the pictures. Do you envision a woman or a man behind the camera?

In 1972, British art historian and writer John Berger made a TV series about the difference between the way artists and advertisers typically represent women, and the way they usually portray men.

Called *Ways of Seeing*, the series showed how much of our cultural imagery has reinforced the idea that "men act and women appear."

Using many examples from a variety of places and times, Berger demonstrated that men are more often shown doing something, while women are more often pictured simply posing for a male audience. Others refer to this as the "male gaze," by which they mean that there's something about the way we paint or photograph women that often assumes the viewer of

> "WE PROVIDE PICTURES OF GIRLS IN THE SAME WAY WE PROVIDE PICTURES OF COOL CARS. IT IS ORNAMENTAL."
> —ALEX BILMES, EDITOR OF ESQUIRE UK

GAZING WITH WORDS

The "male gaze" is usually associated with visual media like photos and paintings, but sometimes it comes through in words as well. Read a gossip site or magazine and notice how often female celebrities are described as "flaunting" or "showing off" their bodies, even if they're wearing ordinary clothes like jeans and a T-shirt.

Meanwhile, interviews and profiles of women tend to spend a lot more time describing their appearance and clothes than similar articles about men, though the woman might be famous for reasons that have nothing to do with her appearance, like being a business owner or a politician.

the image is male. Surprisingly, even a lot of media aimed at female viewers tend to have this point of view—just look at all the sexy images of female models and celebrities in mainstream women's fashion magazines. Women viewing these images might experience the feeling of split personality: they are encouraged to identify with the desirable girl being viewed, as well as with an imagined male viewer.

Being portrayed so often as objects to be looked at—as opposed to people who are doing things—makes women and girls much more aware of themselves as being watched. In the process, they absorb the message that they're being evaluated on the basis of how they look. And often they start to evaluate *themselves* that way, seeing their own bodies in terms of how they please an observer.

EXTREME HEROES

When the GI Joe action figure doll first came out in 1964, he looked like a fit but reasonably normal guy. More recently, he's morphed into a freak show at the circus. The biceps of "GI Joe Extreme," released 34 years later, are bigger than the doll's waist! If they were ratcheted up to human scale, they'd be even larger than the arms of the most massive bodybuilders.

You can see the same effect at work in the evolving images of superheroes. The actors who played Superman and Batman on screen in the 1950s and 1960s look positively doughy compared to the ultra-ripped versions of today. And video game action heroes like Duke Nukem and Ryu from *Street Fighter* are continuing the trend.

So what: they're only games, right? Well, recent studies by psychologists have found that boys and men felt worse about their own bodies after playing games featuring heavily muscled characters.

POSING LIKE *a Girl*

In 2013, a Swedish blogger drew attention to a series of images on the American Apparel website that showed both men and women wearing the company's unisex button-up shirt. The male models wear the shirt tucked into pants, slightly unbuttoned at the neck, with the sleeves rolled up. They're shown leaning casually against a windowsill, or hanging out on a balcony with friends.

Contrast this with the pictures of female models wearing the exact same shirt. Instead of pairing it with pants or a skirt, they wear thong underwear, or no bottoms at all. The shirts are either completely unbuttoned with nothing underneath, or tied high at the waist to show the models' stomachs. And the models pose seductively, glancing over their shoulders with bare bums to the camera, or straddling a chair, or kneeling on a tabletop. The side-by-side images are a striking display of how differently men and women are depicted in advertising and visual media.

The ways women pose in ads, movie posters, and fashion spreads are even more ridiculous if you imagine a man in their place. In 2013, a group of students at the University of Saskatchewan did just that. They created a video (viewable on YouTube)

WHAT IF *GUYS'* BODIES WERE SHOWN LIKE WOMEN'S?

that recreated images from classic and modern ads, only with the gender roles swapped. The reimagined ads showed, among other things, a man reclining on the floor with his bare torso visible under an unbuttoned coat; another leaning over with an energy drink can strapped into his thong; and a third naked on hands and knees, covered in shoes and belts. The effect is more absurd than alluring, inviting viewers to reconsider the original ads featuring women.

WEIGHTY MAGAZINE MESSAGES

Go figure: even though more men than women are overweight, women's magazines emphasize weight loss and body image more than 10 times as often as magazines targeted to guys.

Women's health and fitness magazines tend to focus on weight loss, and workouts with names like "The Bikini Body Booty Routine" that send the message that women only exercise to look good. Men's fitness magazines, meanwhile, are more likely to focus on athletics, building strength, and overall health.

SAYS WHO?

◇◇◇◇◇◇◇◇◇◇◇◇◇◇◇◇◇◇◇◇◇

You don't have to know the history behind the double standard of looking good or be out in the workforce to have experienced it. By high school, the effects are already being felt. Here's how a bunch of 17-year-olds we interviewed see the differences.

GUYS SAY:

We want to look bigger, whereas girls want to look smaller. So we work out and they diet.

Girls worry way more about their outfits, get stressed about what they wear.

Some girls won't date any guys who are under six feet tall.

Most girls are more forgiving of guys' looks than guys are of theirs. Other things are more important to them.

If you're approachable, girls will like you.

Girls feel the need to be in a relationship more than guys, so they're not as picky.

Guys get teased if they go to a tanning salon.

You get known as a pretty boy if you're excessively focused on your looks.

It's okay for girls to admit they spend time on their looks, but it's not cool for guys—we're supposed to look natural.

GIRLS SAY:

We want guys to be slim, toned, but not really built.

We want guys' hair to look good without looking like they've tried to make it look good.

Height is nice—or at least a guy who projects tallness. If he has confidence, that helps.

Girls like guys with amazing eyes that really look at you.

Personality is more important than looks.

Girls like to look at guys with amazing bodies, but often we can't stand those kinds of guys when we get to know them.

Girls berate themselves after eating certain foods, and skip meals.

It's really important for girls to be good-looking.

We always feel we could look better than we do.

POWER
PLAY

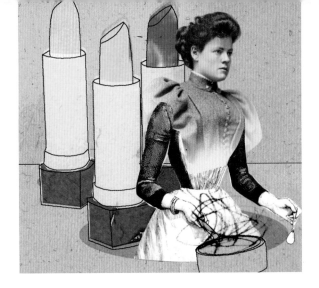

◇◇◇◇◇◇◇◇◇◇◇◇◇◇◇◇◇◇◇◇

When critics slam the media for putting so much emphasis on women's appearances, some people respond by suggesting that if beautiful young women didn't agree to appear in the advertisements that reinforce such messages, the problem would be solved. "It's women's own fault," they argue. "And if women stopped buying fashion mags and makeup, then the magazines and cosmetics companies would go out of business."

It's a solid point. But you can't turn around centuries of emphasis on women's looks overnight. Our attitudes about what's feminine and what's masculine—in terms of appearance and behavior and jobs and responsibilities—are quite entrenched.

Partly it's a power issue. For centuries, women in many societies were treated in an extremely unfair way. They weren't allowed to go to school or decide when or if they wanted to marry. They had very little control over their lives, and were expected to do what their fathers or husbands told them to. Their primary value was defined by their ability to attract and serve their husbands.

Although all cultures depended on women's work (in the home at least), extraordinary emphasis was still also placed on whether or not women lived up to the beauty ideal of the time. The ones who did often gained power as a result. They were sometimes able to exercise more independence and choose who to marry.

Today, of course, we still prize beauty, and beautiful women are very desirable to men. But what's different in the 21st century is that—in the Western world, at least—women and girls have many more choices. Education and work opportunities allow them to be financially independent of men. They might still care about their appearance, but it's no longer the only—or even most important—source of their power.

"A GIRL SHOULD BE TWO THINGS: WHO AND WHAT SHE WANTS." —DESIGNER COCO CHANEL

TALL, DARK, *and* HANDSOME

⬦⬦⬦⬦⬦⬦⬦⬦⬦⬦⬦⬦⬦⬦⬦

As with women, guys with clear skin, thick hair, and toned muscles have typically been preferred over those without.

"I DON'T SEE MYSELF AS EXTREMELY HANDSOME. I JUST FIGURE I CAN CHARM YOU INTO LIKING ME."
—ACTOR WESLEY SNIPES

But throughout the ages, boys and men have also been valued more for things besides their physical appearance. Their earning power, for instance, and their ability to feed their families and put a roof over their heads. Guys with power—whether it came from having land, or money, or followers—looked like good mates, regardless of how physically attractive they were.

Even today, guys who would never be mistaken for a movie star or model are judged to be very desirable if they have other qualities. Power and authority have assisted many ordinary-looking men in being perceived as attractive. And talented male actors or musicians are often seen as sexy, even though without their talent and the power and attention it gets them, they might not make anyone's top 10 list.

So guys may not have to worry as much about whether or not their face and body conform to that of a single male ideal. But the power issue puts a different kind of pressure on them. The kind of job they have and the kinds of things they own can influence whether people judge them to be winners.

NEVER MIND ME—CHECK OUT MY DATE!

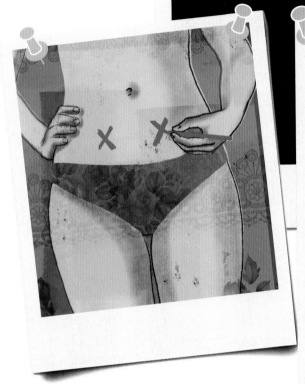

Elle magazine surveyed 59,000 of its male and female readers on the subject of body image. When asked which they would rather have, a perfect body themselves, or a partner with a perfect body, the vast majority of the women chose a perfect body for themselves.

In contrast, the guys were less interested in their own perfection and more interested in having partners whose bodies were perfect.

The power that comes from being beautiful can be a double-edged sword. On the one hand, it can get you noticed. On the other hand, the kind of attention it generates can often be difficult to handle. Being whistled at on the street can make a girl feel good about how she looks, but it can also make her feel vulnerable and threatened. (Even if you view this kind of attention as completely positive, how will it affect your self-esteem if you go out one day and *don't* get whistled at?)

Many women in show business—and some of the guys as well—have stories about the "casting couch": experiences when they received unwanted advances from people higher up in the industry, sometimes with promises of fame attached. These situations can be extremely distressing for young models and performers, and the risk of hurting their careers may keep them from speaking up.

WHISTLE WOES

BEST-BEFORE DATE

◇◇◇◇◇◇◇◇◇◇◇◇◇◇◇◇◇◇◇◇

Two blockbuster movies from 2013 reveal an interesting double standard:
in *Iron Man 3*, 48-year-old Robert Downey Jr. plays the superhero of the title, while in the reboot *Man of Steel*, 48-year-old Diane Lane plays… Superman's mom.

Why are there no female action heroes pushing 50? While men in Hollywood often get to play leading roles well past age 60, women over 35 tend to get cast in supporting parts as moms, or grandmas (sometimes to "children" played by actors who are only a few years younger).

In show business, women have to work a lot harder to stay young-looking, while guys are perceived as being like fine wine: the older they get, the better they are. On top of that, the real-life consequences of

not getting rid of the lines and graying hair that accompany growing older are more serious for women. Although there are some exceptions, the earning potential of female actors, models, and news anchors has a tendency to plummet the minute they start looking like they've hit middle age. The older women we *do* see in the media have often had so many injections, lifts, and tucks that we start to forget what a natural 40- or 60-year-old face actually looks like. And women in the public eye who undergo too-obvious cosmetic procedures are often mocked for having "too much work done" or making their faces unrecognizable.

Things may be changing somewhat, as movie studios and TV networks realize there's a huge audience of women over 40

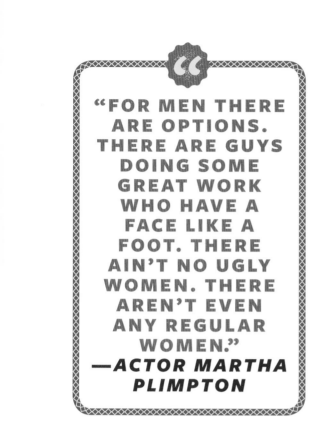

> ## "FOR MEN THERE ARE OPTIONS. THERE ARE GUYS DOING SOME GREAT WORK WHO HAVE A FACE LIKE A FOOT. THERE AIN'T NO UGLY WOMEN. THERE AREN'T EVEN ANY REGULAR WOMEN."
> ## —ACTOR MARTHA PLIMPTON

SCHLUMPY GETS THE GIRL

A strange thing happens to actors in Hollywood: male movie stars get older, but their female love interests all seem to stay the same age.

Craggy-faced, balding, and out-of-shape guys are often paired with female co-stars who are young enough to be their daughters. And even when co-stars are more closely matched in age, TV shows and movies have a tendency to pair guys with women who are way out of their league, looks-wise. In the fantasy world of sitcoms and movies, badly dressed, quirky-looking men often have no trouble at all attracting conventionally hot, thin, impeccably groomed girlfriends and wives.

Of course, in real life these pairings do sometimes happen: men and women both date people who are older or younger, or more or less physically attractive than they are. But when it's nearly always the women who are the younger, hotter ones, it reinforces the perception that women are essentially there for decoration. It tells us that guys can be appealing partners because they're funny, or decent. But girls—even when they have those qualities—must be pretty as well.

who like to see female characters closer to their own age, and who will buy movie tickets and bring in TV ad revenue when they see themselves represented on screen. A handful of older female actors have proved they can headline hit movies, and more and more TV shows are featuring complex, attractive female characters with a few decades of life experience.

Off-screen celebrity romances have also challenged the idea that women over a certain age have passed their best-before date: stars like Halle Berry, Jennifer Lopez, and Mariah Carey have dated or married younger guys. Even so, gossip sites and tabloids often make a big deal out of such relationships, though they usually don't bat an eye when the situation is reversed.

Ripped Bodies
FOR SALE

Until fairly recently, naked men in advertising were as scarce as plain women on TV.

And nobody had even heard of the term "six-pack" to describe a set of abdominal muscles.

Not anymore. Since the 1990s, all sorts of advertisers have jumped on the "Let's exploit men, too!" bandwagon. These days, billboards and magazine ads feature bare-chested male models flashing the kind of muscle-bound physiques that most guys can only dream of having.

And it's not just ads: the video for Carly Rae Jepsen's hit song "Call Me Maybe" was a classic example of what's been termed the "female gaze." It features the singer ogling a good-looking, super-ripped guy stripping off his shirt while mowing the lawn.

Some men are beginning to realize the downside to being compared all the time to images of human perfection—ones that are as difficult and sometimes dangerous for men to achieve as they are for women. Being encouraged to feel insecure about how they measure up physically has consequences: men worry more today than they used to about their bodies; they spend more time and money trying to sculpt themselves into the desirable shape; and some engage in risky behavior like dieting or taking steroids in pursuit of the media-dictated ideal.

What prompted advertisers to start featuring gorgeous male bodies in the ways that they used to only for female bodies?

It has everything to do with wanting to sell more products. Marketing executives figured that if advertising has convinced women for more than 150 years to buy goods they may not need, the same approach could work with guys.

The strategy has paid off. In the past couple of decades, men's spending—of time and money—on personal care products like skin cream and hair gel has grown exponentially. Male grooming products are now one of the fastest-growing sectors of the beauty industry, worth over $80 billion a year worldwide.

DOUBLE
Take

Maybe the double standard is on its way out. What do you think? Are women and girls starting to expect guys to live up to the kind of perfection that they feel guys expect of them? And if so, is this good news?

Some people fantasize about eliminating not just the double standard, but all standards that are based on something other than reality. Then the pressure would be off both sexes. But in the age of saturation advertising, that's hard to imagine. Which is all the more reason to do a reality check every time you're confronted with some claim about how guys or girls should look.

Just to get you started, consider:

Women and girls have way more choices today than ever before. This means more opportunity to make decisions—on the beauty front and elsewhere—that are right for you, no matter what anybody else is doing.

Gender-flipping can be an eye-opening exercise when looking at movies, TV, and ads. Imagine a guy being portrayed in a way that is commonplace for girls.

Regardless of what advertisers claim or imply, personality plays a big role in determining a person's attractiveness.

Advertisers make money from the personal insecurities of both men and women. The images they produce are designed to distort our perceptions of human ideals in order to sell us products.

Men can be considered good-looking with silver hair and lined faces, so why not women?

BEAUTY
Power

✧✧✧✧✧✧✧✧✧

WE REFER TO GORGEOUS PEOPLE

as "stunning"—as if merely looking at them will knock us out. We say they are "bewitching"—as if their beauty has magical powers. We call them "ravishing"— as if their physical appearance were capable of carrying us off by force.

✧✧✧✧✧✧✧✧✧✧✧✧✧

In other words, we attribute all sorts of power to people just because of how their faces are arranged and their bodies are put together.

Attributed power can translate into real power. And throughout history, individuals have taken advantage of that power to get what they want.

On a larger scale, too, groups of people have used the power of beauty— as *they* defined it—to advance their interests at the expense of others. Sometimes this has been unconscious, and sometimes deliberate.

SOMETIMES
BEAUTY CAN BE A
POWERFUL WEAPON.

DIFFERENT SHADES

Even though the dominant images of beauty in the early 1900s were unmistakably white, Madame C.J. Walker created and began marketing a line of cosmetics for black women in 1905. In the process, she became America's first African-American female millionaire business owner.

Over a century later, you can still see racial biases at the makeup counter: cosmetics companies often label products with names like "nude," "natural," or "flesh," which usually translates to a peachy shade that's only "nude" or "flesh" in color if you happen to be white. And some makeup products' ranges don't even include colors to match darker skin tones.

BATTLES
ON THE
Beauty Front

◇◇◇◇◇◇◇◇◇◇◇◇◇◇◇◇◇◇◇◇

All through history, people of different races have tended to celebrate as beautiful the things that set their physical appearance apart from others. When Europeans colonized America, Africa, and parts of Asia, starting in the 15th century and continuing into the 20th, they sought to conquer the original inhabitants and claim the land as their own. In the process, they denigrated Native American, African, and Asian people as less civilized and pointed to the indigenous peoples' skin color to justify their bigotry. Ever since, the dominant images of "beautiful" people in the West have tended to feature fair-skinned Caucasians.

In addition, the African, Asian, Hispanic, and Native American faces most likely to be portrayed in the media as beautiful have tended to be those that most resembled white people's—either because of the lightness of their complexions or the shape of their facial features.

But things are changing. North American popular culture is broadening its definition of what's attractive to reflect the greater diversity of people who live here, and to appeal to a global audience. Although white actors and models still get a disproportionate amount of camera time, magazines, TV shows, and movies now regularly feature people of color. Asian, African-American, Hispanic, and mixed-race performers have helped to send the message that beauty has many different faces, and not all of them are white. And as the picture of beauty changes, attitudes shift along with it.

> "A FEW TIMES I GOT EXCUSED BY DESIGNERS WHO TOLD ME, 'WE ALREADY FOUND ONE BLACK GIRL. WE DON'T NEED YOU ANYMORE.' I FELT VERY DISCOURAGED. WHEN SOMEONE TELLS YOU, 'WE DON'T WANT YOU BECAUSE WE ALREADY HAVE ONE OF YOUR KIND,' IT'S REALLY SAD."
> —MODEL CHANEL IMAN

WASPS IN CHARGE

The acronym WASP is short for "White Anglo-Saxon Protestant." In North America today, it's often used in a derogatory way to dismiss someone as being conservative and unfairly privileged. Historically, people of WASP background, whose ancestors came from northern Europe, have had more money, power, and influence here than people who came from other parts of the world. Their control of business and the media meant they got to decide all sorts of things, including who could be called beautiful.

When beauty pageants were first created in North America in the late 19th century, only white women were allowed to enter. In 1945, when the Miss America pageant was won by Bess Myerson, there was a big uproar. Although she was white, she was Jewish, and therefore not a "WASP."

But Myerson used the attention that winning the pageant gave her to challenge bigotry. "You can't be beautiful and hate," she said.

EXTREME
Makeovers

◇◇◇◇◇◇◇◇◇◇◇◇◇◇◇◇◇◇◇◇◇◇◇◇◇◇◇◇◇◇◇◇

Many traits traditionally seen as beautiful in Western society, from skin color to hair texture to the shape of facial features, were influenced by racist and anti-Semitic attitudes.

Under colonialism, slavery, and segregation, people of color who more closely resembled the prevailing WASP standard often received better treatment, and encountered less discrimination. Unable to change society, some changed their appearances instead, buying products like skin-whitening creams and hair straighteners.

Today, attitudes have come a long way. People can choose to straighten their hair, brighten their skin, or even get cosmetic surgery simply because that's the look they're after, not because they're trying to look more "white." But it's still worth examining what forces led us to see certain traits or features as more attractive than others.

Nose Woes

Noses come in a variety of shapes and sizes, but for decades the WASP button nose ruled them all. As waves of immigrants came to North America in the 20th century, many people of Jewish, Greek, and Italian descent sought nose jobs in an effort to "pass" as WASP and be accepted by the people with power.

Since 2000, cosmetic surgeons have reported a sharp decline in overall demand for nose jobs, and for well-off Jewish teens, they're no longer the "rite of passage" they used to be. At the same time, however, some surgeons say the procedure has become more popular among Hispanic and Asian Americans.

Western Eyes

After World War II, when discrimination against the Japanese was at an all-time high, many Asian Americans sought surgery to alter their eyes to make them look more Western. These days, eyes with a "double lid" (as opposed to the naturally uncreased "single lids" of many Asians) continue to be seen by some as markers of beauty.

The procedure is controversial: in 2013, when TV host Julie Chen admitted she'd had eyelid surgery early in her career, under pressure from her boss to look "less Asian," she received both support and criticism for her choice.

Lightening Up

Cosmetic surgery couldn't help African Americans avoid discrimination, but marketers still found ways to profit by encouraging them to come as close to the "white" beauty ideal as possible. Today, huge cosmetics companies sell skin-lightening creams with names like "White Perfect" and "Fair & Lovely" to people all over the world.

Unfortunately, these creams often contain harsh ingredients that can cause permanent skin damage. In India, where skin-whitening treatments outsell Coca-Cola, Bollywood actress Nandita Das took a stand by becoming the face of the Dark Is Beautiful campaign, which challenges the harmful idea that fair skin is superior.

Hair Hassles

Companies have made a lot of money by convincing women of color that there's something wrong with the natural texture of their hair. The African-American hair care industry sells $9 billion worth of products a year, including everything from weaves and hot irons to "relaxers" (creams designed to straighten curls, that contain a corrosive acid so strong it can burn your scalp).

Straight hair has become so much the norm in fashion media that most people see it as simply a style choice, not as a way of valuing the look of one ethnicity over others. Still, a few African-American stars—like the singer Solange Knowles, who claims she used to spend $40,000 a year on hair treatments—have made headlines by embracing their natural hair and wearing afros, dreads, cornrows, or short styles.

SIZE *BIAS*

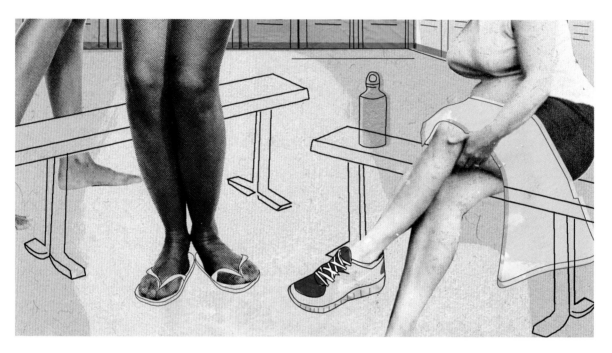

One form of beauty discrimination that affects all races and genders is based on weight.

While in the real world, people find a variety of body shapes and sizes appealing, in the media, plus-sized guys and girls are usually depicted as unattractive, food-obsessed, and unlikely to get a date. Even extremely good-looking people with fuller figures are often portrayed as less beautiful than thinner ones.

This bias translates into a lack of power. Studies have shown that overweight kids and teens are more likely to be bullied, and less likely to be accepted to prestigious universities, while adults who are perceived as being fat are much less likely to be hired, promoted, or paid a competitive salary. And although there are laws that prevent discrimination against people on the basis of their race, religion, gender, or age, only a few places in North America have laws to protect the overweight.

The desire to lose weight, or the fear of gaining weight, drives some people to extreme behavior. Many girls and women become desperate to achieve the media's narrow body image ideals and end up severely restricting what they eat, going overboard with exercise, or purging their bodies of food by using laxatives or vomiting. Some even post "thinspiration" or "thinspo" images of skinny models on social media sites as a way of expressing their obsession with losing weight, and encouraging others to do the same.

Media images and social pressures on girls to be slender may encourage anorexia and bulimia, but they're not entirely to blame. Eating disorders are a form of mental illness with a lot of different causes, and they usually lack simple explanations. Many girls who develop eating disorders feel that they have little or no impact on other people or on events in their lives; controlling their food intake or body shape becomes a way of exercising power.

The "power" that women and girls gain through disordered eating is a complete illusion. Instead, the conditions seriously weaken them, and their self-perceptions become so severely distorted that their controlling behavior ends up threatening their health.

Guys are increasingly affected by eating disorders, too, although not nearly as often. But because anorexia and bulimia are so often seen as "girl" problems, boys and men suffering from these conditions are sometimes too embarrassed to seek treatment, so the actual number of cases may be larger than what's reported.

SIZE IS JUST a NUMBER

Clothing sizes for both women and men have gotten smaller over the years, a trend that's been termed "vanity sizing." The same dress that would have been labeled a size 14 in the 1930s would have been downsized to a size 8 in the 1960s, and—believe it or not—to a size zero in many stores today. What's more, sizes vary widely among brands and stores. A magazine report found that in one store, the waistband on a pair of men's pants labeled "36 inches" actually measured a full 5 inches more!

Why do companies do this? There's evidence people spend more on clothes if they can wear a smaller size. Clothing manufacturers are profiting from many people's desire to be thinner, even if the downside is that you have to try on three different sizes because one store's size 12 is another's size 16. And where do you go after zero? Some fashion designers have had to invent double-zero sizes for the truly tiny, because their regular sizes have been so inflated.

SIZE	BUST	WAIST	HIP
XXS	31.5	24	34
XS	33.5	26	36
S	35.5	28	38
M	37.5	30	40
L	40.5	33	43
XL	44	36	46.5
XXL	46	37.5	48.5

EFFECTS *of* DISORDERED EATING

ANOREXIA

loss of menstrual periods in girls and women
weakness
osteoporosis or bone damage
hair loss, pigment changes
vitamin and mineral deficiencies
stunted growth
starvation and death

BULIMIA

gastrointestinal damage
iron and other nutritional deficiencies
diarrhea
kidney damage
damage to teeth
damage to esophagus
heart attack and death

The Goldilocks
PROBLEM

◇◇◇◇◇◇◇◇◇◇◇◇◇◇◇◇◇◇

For women in the media, and the tabloids and gossip sites that obsessively scrutinize them, it seems like there's about a three-pound acceptable margin between "dangerously thin" and "shockingly chubby." It could be called the Goldilocks Problem: the same publications that shout "too fat" at the tiniest hint of celebrity weight gain will turn around and cry "too thin" when someone appears to have lost weight. Of course, the reason they do this is to sell magazines and generate page views. For some reason, *Celebrity Appears to Be a Healthy, Average Size!* doesn't have quite the same headline appeal.

Skinny guys and girls don't experience anything close to the kind of discrimination obese people face, but they often have to deal with rude remarks about their weight, or comments that they should "eat a sandwich." Thin people are sometimes assumed to have an eating disorder when they might just be naturally thin, or have lost weight because they've been ill or stressed.

Health concerns are often used to justify discrimination against fat people, too; some argue that accepting and celebrating bigger body sizes actually encourages overeating and other unhealthy behavior. News reports often remind us of the dangers of obesity, while portraying overweight people in an extremely negative way: shot from the back or side with their heads cropped out of the frame, wearing ill-fitting clothing, or eating junk food.

In fact, some studies have shown that "chubby" people actually live *longer* on average than normal-weight or underweight people, and that even obese people who eat well and are active can be healthy, whether or not they lose weight. Focusing on looks as opposed to health, however, has the effect of making overweight people ashamed of their bodies, which might discourage them from actually doing things that would keep them healthy, like exercising and eating nutritious food.

If you feel tempted to make a remark about someone's size (whether it's someone you know, or a celebrity on a computer screen), just remember:

◉ **Whether a person is fat, thin, or in between, it can be very hard to tell from their appearance whether or not they're healthy, or how much they eat. The size of your body is influenced by a lot of things, from genetics to metabolism to medications, only some of which are under your control.**

◉ **If you think someone does have an eating disorder, keep in mind that he or she is suffering from an illness, and needs compassion and support, not judgment.**

REALITY vs TELEVISION

A study in the *American Journal of Public Health* found:

1 in 2 American women are overweight or obese

1 in 8 female TV characters are overweight or obese

1 in 20 American women are underweight

1 in 3 female TV characters are underweight

LOOKS LAWS

In the not-so-distant past, some American cities imposed fines on people who were considered unsightly by those in power. For instance, from 1966 to 1974, a subsection of Chicago's vagrancy law dictated that people who were "diseased, maimed, mutilated, or in any way deformed so as to be an unsightly or disgusting object" could be fined for appearing in public.

The attitudes that led to the creation of such laws are shocking today. Now we use the legal system to protect people with disabilities from discrimination and ensure they're full participants in every aspect of society.

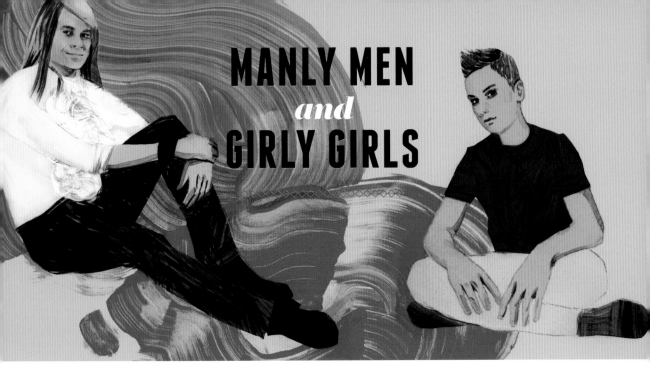

MANLY MEN *and* GIRLY GIRLS

Traditional ideas about the roles of men and women also have power over our definitions of beauty.

Men who have physical characteristics traditionally thought of as "masculine," like muscular bodies and strong jawlines, and women with stereotypically "feminine" characteristics—long hair, soft facial features, curvy figures—have usually been judged more attractive than people whose appearance, dress, or grooming has qualities associated with the opposite gender. Often this stems from negative attitudes toward gay and transgender people (who identify with a different gender from the one they were born with), or toward anyone else who doesn't fit neatly into conventional gender roles. Guys who wear makeup, for instance, and women who cut their hair very short or wear men's-style clothing, have often faced discrimination,

threats, and even violence because of the way they look. If they are portrayed in the mainstream media at all, it's often as strange or unattractive, or as people to be laughed at. And these attitudes start early: little boys get bullied at school for wearing pink, and girls with no interest in frilly dresses are called "tomboys."

The increased visibility of gay and transgender people in North American society has broadened people's view of the many different ways men and women can look and dress. The world of high fashion, which has traditionally employed many gay people, often celebrates the androgynous look—a style that isn't identifiably masculine or feminine, but could be interpreted either way. Some designers even use transgender models to challenge ideals and attract attention. Yet mainstream movies, TV shows, and magazines still very rarely break out of the manly-man and girly-girl mold.

THE FASHION POLICE

In days gone by, the ruling elites in some countries actually passed laws designed to prevent the lower classes from wearing specific fabrics and styles:

In both 17th-century France and colonial Massachusetts, only wealthy people were allowed to wear adornments such as gold embroidery and lace.

At one time, certain residents of Venice were forbidden to wear more than a single strand of pearls.

In Japan, elaborately decorated kimonos and fine silks were reserved for the nobility.

But the laws always bombed. The people who were prohibited from wearing the restricted clothing or jewelry would either disregard the restrictions completely or they'd come up with their own takes on the fashionable items.

BRANDED BEAUTY

If some people risk their health attempting to control their bodies, many others risk their finances trying to win at the wardrobe game.

More than anyone else, teenagers are affected by the brand-name beauty wars, in which clothes become essential weapons.

Whether it's Adidas shoes, Hollister hoodies, or True Religion jeans, often what matters in clothing is not the color or the shape but the name. Buying the right brand is like silently informing everyone around you that you're savvy enough to know what's in. The chosen brand embodies the irresistible promise of automatic cool to anyone who has the cash to buy it.

But what about those who don't?

The pressure to buy the right brand names is so harsh that many kids whose families

can't afford expensive clothes feel compelled to get part-time jobs just so they can dress well around other kids. They trade having time to hang out with their friends for making the money necessary to have the right clothes to hang out in.

Of course, the real power in this beauty equation is held by the brand makers themselves. They're the ones who get rich as a result. Consider the range in price for a pair of jeans. The cost of the denim material, thread, and zipper or buttons is often the same, whether the jeans are made by a high-end fashion designer or a discount chain. But you can pay less than $30 for a bargain brand, or 20 times that price—over $600—to advertise the Gucci name across your tush.

Sometimes it's smarter to pay a bit more for clothes if they're better quality, because they're likely to last longer and save you

money in the long run. Clothes made in the US or Canada also cost more than those produced using cheap labor overseas. But if you buy luxury labels, keep in mind that a big part of what you're paying for is the advertising that made you think the brand was so desirable in the first place.

CELEBRITY CHIC

When stars affiliate themselves with certain beauty products or fashion brands, people are not only more likely to buy the brands, but to pay more money for them.

But it's worth asking: do wealthy actors and singers with teams of personal stylists really use the drugstore shampoos they endorse in ads? Or wear Old Navy when they're not being filmed for a TV commercial promoting the company's clothes?

THE
INDIVIDUAL
Copycat

Making the right style statement is a bit of a balancing act. You may want to fit in, to be seen as wearing the brands and styles that have been approved by your crowd. Then again, what you wear and do to your hair are expressions of your individuality—you don't want to be a clone.

When it comes to looking good, there's always been some tension between innovation and imitation. One person or group comes up with a trend that they hope will distinguish them. If it's distinctive, interesting, or beautiful enough, others admire it. But when they succeed in copying the trend and it gets adopted by many people, it loses its value and is no longer so cool. Then the trendsetters have to create a new look to re-establish the fact that they are, indeed, different. That look, too, gets copied, and the whole cycle begins all over again.

For instance, other than earlobes, piercing wasn't a very popular practice when punks in the 1970s began piercing their faces and bodies. Now it's become much more mainstream, and because lots of people are doing it, it's not considered nearly as edgy anymore. The same cyclical process happens with everything from skinny jeans to neon nail polish. What comes in will eventually go out. And whether it will make a comeback someday is anybody's guess.

> "ALWAYS REMEMBER THAT YOU ARE ABSOLUTELY UNIQUE. JUST LIKE EVERYONE ELSE."
> —ANTHROPOLOGIST MARGARET MEAD

DOUBLE
Take

The definition of beauty—in skin color, in body shape, in hair and clothing styles—has become a lot broader and more diverse than it used to be. One flip through a current fashion magazine proves that there's no longer a cookie-cutter mold. And as groups previously excluded from power—people of color, gay people, people with disabilities—have won rights and gained positions of influence, they have also influenced the images of beauty we see.

That might be hard to appreciate when mainstream media still presents an overwhelmingly light-skinned, thin, straight-haired beauty ideal that reflects established systems of power. But in all sorts of places, from blogs to fashion runways, people who have been told they don't fit society's definition of beautiful are turning the tables, and proving old stereotypes wrong.

So this chapter's reflections are:

Enhancing your assets and downplaying your flaws doesn't have to mean erasing your individuality or buying in to the mainstream look.

There's no one definition of beautiful anymore; increasing diversity means more choice and lots of room for expressing yourself in different ways.

Beauty may wield power, but it's hardly absolute.

Why pay extra for brand names unless you really love the clothes? Brand labels really just tell people how much you paid for what you're wearing.

Opportunity
or
KNOCKS?

✧✧✧✧✧✧✧✧✧✧✧✧

IN A WORLD WHERE FIRST
impressions count, it's hard not to believe that looking good smooths your way in life.

✧✧✧✧✧✧✧✧✧✧✧✧

It certainly seems easier to get picked for the cheerleading squad or voted most crush-worthy at school if your reflection in the mirror says "model material." And shopping for clothes or showing up for gym class in shorts may be easier if you're slim as opposed to overweight.

Yet all sorts of people who aren't classically good-looking achieve great things in the world, and live happy, personally rewarding lives. So what do we really know about the advantages of being beautiful?

BEAUTY MIGHT OPEN A DOOR, *BUT WHAT COMES NEXT?*

GUILTY!

If you're heading to court, it usually pays to be good-looking. Many studies over the years have shown that juries tend to convict attractive defendants less often than those considered unattractive, and give them lighter sentences.

But other studies show that under certain circumstances, very attractive people are more likely to be convicted and punished for crimes than unattractive people. Faced with fictional cases of people accused of swindling others out of their money, juries in a mock trial were inclined to believe that defendants described as good-looking possessed the ability to charm innocent victims. They were more likely to judge such defendants guilty as a result. An experiment that used mock cases of women accused of killing their husbands found a similar outcome.

PLEASING
Impressions

If two guys walk into a room and one of them looks like an underwear model and the other looks like Fred, the man who lives down the street, it's common sense that the gorgeous guy will attract more immediate notice.

Some research backs this up. In one study, two women were placed by the side of the road beside cars with flat tires. Drivers passing by were more likely to slow down and help the more attractive one.

Of course, when it comes to romance, beauty genes are no guarantee that sparks will fly and you'll fall in love. But they may increase the likelihood of someone you just met asking you out to a movie, or responding, "Yes, I'd love to" when you invite them to a party.

> "PEOPLE ALWAYS ASK ME, 'YOU HAVE SO MUCH CONFIDENCE. WHERE DID THAT COME FROM?' IT CAME FROM ME. ONE DAY I DECIDED THAT I WAS BEAUTIFUL, AND SO I CARRIED OUT MY LIFE AS IF I WAS A BEAUTIFUL GIRL."
> —ACTOR GABOUREY SIDIBE

The
CONFIDENCE QUOTIENT

◇◇

Beyond the obvious advantages are some other not so obvious ones.

In addition to making a good impression because their faces or bodies are appealing, good-looking people are often more confident than the average person. Maybe it's because they don't feel awkward the way people who are self-conscious or unhappy about their looks sometimes do. Beautiful people—at least to the rest of us—seem to just naturally fit in, no effort required.

Studies show they're also more likely to feel that they have control over their lives—they see themselves choosing and directing what happens to them, as opposed to having to respond to situations and people around them. But what is ironic is that beautiful people often don't attribute much influence to circumstance, despite the fact that the circumstance of being born beautiful can have a big impact on how they're treated by others.

The confidence and sense of control that they feel also translates into a greater sense of self-importance. In one experiment, people were kept waiting while the person who was supposed to be serving them talked on the phone. The really attractive

individuals became impatient much more quickly than the less attractive people did.

Of course, great looks aren't the only source of confidence. People feel good about themselves and project self-assurance based on everything from their athletic or artistic ability to their intelligence or interpersonal skills.

As much as anything else, the research suggests that being treated well has an enormous effect on how people feel about themselves, no matter what they look like.

THE UPS AND DOWNS OF BEAUTY:

A Guide for Gorgeous People

◇◇◇◇◇◇◇◇◇◇◇◇◇◇◇◇◇◇◇

Lucky you—you were born beautiful! But don't start celebrating yet: studies have shown that for every advantage your looks give you, there are probably a few disadvantages, too. Consider...

Your personality...

How others see you...

As a child...

At school...

At work...

With friends...

In love...

When you look in the mirror...

UPS

DOWNS

You're probably more confident than the average person. High five!	How do we put this? You also possibly think quite highly of yourself. (Or maybe this only applies to all those *other* gorgeous people, not *you*.)
Your good looks give you a kind of halo: they make many people think you must have other great qualities, like being interesting, smart, successful, and fun. (No pressure, just be yourself!)	Some people might assume you're conceited, shallow, unintelligent, or untalented. They may think you don't have to work hard, as you get everything because of your looks. (Unfair!)
If you were an especially cute baby, you probably got more smiles and attention from adults than the average baby would.	Cute babies don't always turn out to be cute teenagers; yet, some awkward kids grow up to be models.
Teachers may give you more attention and better grades than your equally smart but less attractive classmates. They're also more likely to excuse your misbehavior.	Don't think you can totally coast by on your looks. It's been shown that your classmates with great personalities, and those who are tidy and well-groomed, have the advantage over you in terms of grades.
You're often at an advantage when applying for jobs, and you're more likely to get promoted and paid a higher salary than equally qualified people judged less attractive. In fact, you can expect to earn 10 to 15 percent more than your plainer coworkers.	Watch out for jealous HR managers! Your beguiling looks might be a disadvantage if the person in charge of hiring is the same gender as you. And if you're female and pretty, you're much less likely to get hired for traditionally male-dominated jobs.
You're probably popular and have lots of friends. Some people will want to hang out with you just so they will appear more attractive and popular themselves.	Sometimes being beautiful can be lonely: potential friends might see you as unapproachable, or they might act jealous or defensive around you.
Everyone wants to date you. You collect phone numbers left and right. You could go out with someone different every night if you wanted to.	Or maybe you hardly ever get asked out because people are intimidated by your good looks. Maybe they assume you must be in such high demand they'll have no chance, and your average-cute best friend gets all the attention instead.
Hey, you're gorgeous, right? No worrying about zits or frizzy hair—you can leave that to mere mortals.	Or do you worry *more* about how you look than the average person, because your appearance is the prism through which others see you, and that has shaped the way you see yourself?

THE POWER OF
FLIRTING

No doubt you've witnessed or experienced the power of flirting.

A guy gives you a second look and it puts a bounce in your step. A girl speaks to you in an intimate way and you're more inclined to respond in kind. Lots of people learn to use the art of flirtation to their advantage, whether or not they're beautiful. And the personality displayed in having a sense of humor or making a witty reply can itself make a person more attractive.

One study had women and men who didn't know each other speak on the phone.

When the men were given photos of beautiful women and told, "This is who you'll be speaking with," researchers noticed that they tried harder and were bolder and funnier than when they were speaking to women they believed to be less attractive.

The women responded to the men who thought they were attractive by becoming bolder, more animated, and more confident themselves. Treated as if they *were* interesting and exciting, they actually *became* more interesting and exciting—a kind of self-fulfilling prophecy.

Pretty-Person JOBS

◇◇◇◇◇◇◇◇◇◇◇◇◇◇◇◇◇◇

Have you ever visited a trendy clothing store or restaurant and thought, "Everyone working here looks like they've just stepped out of a catalogue"?

It's probably no accident. Pretty people have been shown to have an advantage in many job situations, all other factors (like intelligence and work ethic) being equal. But certain workplaces are up front about hiring *only* good-looking, young people, in an effort to create an alluring "brand image" that will attract customers, and their money.

Some clothing stores and restaurants, for instance, have "Look Policies" with strict rules about their employees' appearance and grooming, and have admitted to throwing out the resumés of applicants they consider unattractive. If they do hire less-attractive or overweight people, they'll often stick them in the back of the store stacking shelves or in the kitchen washing dishes, where they can't be seen. (In 2004, one clothing chain was forced to pay a $50-million settlement after being sued by Hispanic, black, and Asian employees

who said they were forced to work in back rooms because they didn't fit the white, preppy look the company was trying to promote.)

Outside of local legislation in a few North American cities, there are no laws to prevent employers from hiring (or not hiring) people on the basis of their beauty, unless racial, gender, or age discrimination is also involved. Of course, it makes sense that looks matter for certain jobs, like modeling or sometimes acting. But there's no way that having perfectly straight teeth and shiny hair makes you more skilled at ringing up the price on a shirt, or balancing dessert plates on your arm.

IS IT FAIR TO HIRE PEOPLE *FOR THEIR LOOKS?*

HEIGHT MATTERS

◇◇◇◇◇◇◇◇◇◇◇◇◇◇◇◇◇◇

Even if you have no desire to shoot hoops or walk a runway, it turns out that the "tall" part of "tall, dark, and handsome" translates into better earning power.

Why? Experts believe it all comes down to assumptions. Taller people are no smarter or more competent than shorter people; we just imagine they must be, based on their height. This doesn't mean that those who are short in stature can't also become very successful, but they probably have to work harder to prove themselves than their tall colleagues do.

Average Height:

6′0″	
5′6″	
5′0″	
4′6″	
4′0″	
3′6″	
3′0″	
2′6″	
2′0″	
1′6″	
1′0″	

AMERICAN MALE CEOS:*
58% ARE 6′0″+
* in the 500 largest companies

AMERICAN MEN:
15% ARE 6′0″+

$789/YEAR:
EXTRA AMOUNT TALL PEOPLE EARN FOR EVERY INCH THEY ARE ABOVE AVERAGE HEIGHT

ONLY SKIN DEEP

◇◇◇◇◇◇◇◇◇◇◇◇◇◇◇◇◇◇◇

The bottom line on beauty advantages is this: attractive people do have a bit of an edge over those who are less attractive.

But beauty is only one variable in what happens in a person's life. Looks are no guarantee of happiness or success. In fact, sometimes beauty can work against you in unexpected ways.

Even though we make some positive assumptions about attractive people without knowing them, a person's beauty can also have a negative impact on how we rate their integrity, sensitivity, or concern for others. In fact, we sometimes assume gorgeous faces belong to people who are conceited or self-absorbed. Apparently the fairy-tale messages about beauty being only skin deep weren't completely wasted on us after all!

Good-looking people are less likely to get asked by others for help, although it's not clear why. Maybe people are intimidated by their beauty or assume that they're too self-important to help others. It may be an advantage not to be asked for favors all the time, but life could be lonely if everyone finds you unapproachable.

easy come, easy go

Because youthfulness is a key aspect of our culture's beauty ideal, many gorgeous people eventually start to notice that they don't receive as much attention as they get older.

This can be devastating. The aging process brings not only changes to their physical appearance, but also a shift in the number of compliments and opportunities they receive. If you've become really attached to being appreciated for how you look, it hits you hard when the compliments stop. Some good-looking people don't invest enough energy in developing other assets or strengths, and the realization that the attention is now focused on a whole new crop of gorgeous teens or 20-somethings can result in depression and eroded self-esteem.

In some ways, growing older can be much easier for people who never thought of themselves as beautiful in the first place.

> **"THE PROBLEM WITH BEAUTY IS THAT IT'S LIKE BEING BORN RICH AND GETTING PROGRESSIVELY POORER."**
> **—'80S SOAP OPERA STAR JOAN COLLINS**

"DON'T HATE ME
Because I'm Beautiful"

Beauty has been called "an unearned advantage."

In contrast to the hard work and effort people invest in developing a skill, running a successful business, or helping others, merely tumbling out of your mother's womb with a genetic package that's sure to turn heads does seem unfair. It's easy to resent the opportunities or attention another person gets because of something they had nothing to do with. And advertisers that invite us to compare our own bodies and faces to the impossibly buff and beautiful ones they use to sell products play a big role in inspiring feelings of inadequacy.

The "Don't hate me…" line was used in an advertising campaign for Pantene shampoo. By asking viewers not to hate the woman whose image appeared in it, the ad actually encouraged resentment by bringing up the idea in the first place. Without the slogan, it probably wouldn't have occurred to most viewers of the ad to hate the woman. What's more, the slogan implies that we *should* be jealous because, unlike the model, we're *not* beautiful—an unfortunate situation that could of course be remedied if we just bought the shampoo.

Living in a world that values good looks, many people do feel jealous of those who are more attractive. That's understandable. But the result is that beautiful women sometimes have a harder time making friends with other women. Researchers call this the "contrast effect." The idea is that since nobody likes to be compared unfavorably with someone else, hanging out with a hot friend causes you to think you look bad in comparison.

On the other hand, would being gorgeous make up for having to worry about whether or not people will hate or avoid you for it?

Beautiful DISADVANTAGES

◇◇◇◇◇◇◇◇◇◇◇◇◇◇◇◇◇◇◇◇

Many women have complained about the career obstacles they've faced because of their appearance. Attractive or young-looking women can feel that they're not taken seriously at their jobs, or that they're dismissed as "pretty faces" without any talent or ability. In 2010, a woman in New York City was even fired from her job as a banker, because, she claimed, her bosses said her beauty was too distracting.

Even in the movie business, where good looks are practically essential for stardom, having them can be a handicap. Sometimes especially beautiful performers find that directors underestimate their acting abilities, and cast them in limited roles that require them to look good and not much else. For a number of actors, including Charlize Theron, Brad Pitt, and Halle Berry, it was only when they disguised or toned down their beauty to play less glamorous parts that they gained recognition and awards for their talent as well as their looks.

BIMBOS AND HIMBOS

You probably recognize this character from many movies, TV shows, and ads: the airhead hottie, who gets by on great looks but doesn't have much going on upstairs. Implied in the stereotype is the idea that brains and beauty are incompatible.

The truth is, of course, that good-looking people are just as likely to be smart, or not smart, as everyone else. But many people still unconsciously assume that a man or woman can't be both gorgeous *and* intelligent.

> "THOUGH BEAUTY GIVES YOU A WEIRD SENSE OF ENTITLEMENT, IT'S RATHER FRIGHTENING AND THREATENING TO HAVE OTHERS ASCRIBE SUCH IMPORTANCE TO SOMETHING YOU KNOW YOU'RE JUST RENTING FOR A WHILE."
> —*ACTOR CANDICE BERGEN*

MORE THAN JUST A
Pretty Package

People who are used to getting positive attention for their looks alone sometimes find it hard to trust that others are really interested in more than their physical exterior.

Like most of us, they want to be appreciated for their personal qualities and feelings, too, or the talents they've worked hard to develop. When people are constantly telling you you're beautiful, it might make you question whether other things about you matter to them as well. You might wonder if they see you for who you actually are, or if they're just dazzled by your appearance.

For sure, when you're beautiful, you benefit from the outsized importance our society places on looks. But it can also be hard for you to be valued for anything else. As problems go, you might think, "bring it on," but like lots of things in life—money, fame, intellectual brilliance—the benefits of beauty are not as straightforward as they might seem on the surface.

> "BEING A SEX SYMBOL IS A HEAVY LOAD TO CARRY."
> —SILENT FILM ACTOR CLARA BOW

DOUBLE
Take

As much as we might wish otherwise, the truth is, life isn't always fair, and—just as you may have suspected—beautiful people do have some advantages. But studies suggest that those advantages are not really significant when compared to the kinds of things you actually have control over, like your interests, your personality, or your attitude toward the world. So the following points are mostly about experimenting with that knowledge:

Try treating *everyone* as if they are beautiful—whether you consider them so or not. Do they become more confident, dynamic, and interesting in response? And do you?

As big a factor as beauty is in our world, the truth is that *how* you approach your life will have a much bigger impact on where it takes you than what you look like.

Most of us probably don't *intend* to treat good-looking people differently from anyone else, but the evidence shows that a lot of the time, we do. With that in mind, start noticing how you respond to people's packaging, and what kind of unconscious assumptions you make about them because of how they look.

Competition

24/7

◇◇◇◇◇◇◇◇◇◇◇

THERE'S NO FORMAL ENTRY

**requirement for the beauty contest of life;
just being born puts you on the stage,
whether you want to be judged or not.**

◇◇◇◇◇◇◇◇◇◇◇

Every day, in different ways, we're encouraged to compare, rank, and evaluate people based on their looks. Maybe it's an online poll of whether someone is "hot or not," or a modeling competition on TV. It could be a fashion magazine asking, "Which celebrity wore it better?" or a lunchroom debate about who has the best hair in school. Or maybe it's the unspoken assessments we all make while walking to class, or clicking through friends' photos online.

Is there any escape from the rating game?

NOT ALL BEAUTY CONTESTS COME WITH *TIARAS AND PRIZES.*

ANCIENT *BEAUTY* RIVALRIES

◇◇◇◇◇◇◇◇◇◇◇◇◇◇◇◇◇◇

The first recorded beauty competition dates back to Roman mythology. It illustrates the seductive powers of beauty—and the pitfalls of judging it.

The Party

Jupiter, the king of the gods, invited all the gods to a feast. Eris, a troublemaking goddess, was left off the guest list. She showed up anyway, and when they wouldn't let her in, she tossed an apple into the banquet hall, proclaiming that the most beautiful woman should pick it up.

The Fight

Three goddesses—Juno, Minerva, and Venus—all claimed to be the best looking. Realizing (wisely) that he'd get himself in trouble by picking one over the others, Jupiter delegated the task to Paris— an ordinary mortal.

The Bribes

The contending beauties used their powers to persuade Paris (the beginning of a long tradition of corruption in beauty contests!). Juno promised to make him rich, Minerva pledged to give him wisdom and bravery, and Venus promised to arrange for him to marry the most beautiful woman in the world. This is where Helen of Troy— remember her from chapter 1?—comes in.

The Judgment

Paris was more taken with the idea of having a gorgeous girl on his arm than he was with untold riches or power, so he declared Venus to be the best looking of the three and got Helen as his prize. You may recall how well that turned out— the two lovers running away together started the Trojan War!

BATHING
Beauties

◇◇◇◇◇◇◇◇◇◇◇◇◇◇◇◇◇◇

The first real-world beauty competitions weren't nearly as dramatic as the mythological ones.

In the medieval era, English festivals such as the May Day celebrations began the practice of selecting "queens" who served as symbols of the rebirth of spring. But the real precursor to the kind of organized contest we associate with Miss America or Miss World didn't show up until the 1850s.

Around this time, P.T. Barnum (of Barnum & Bailey circus fame) operated a popular museum in New York City, hosting all kinds of "national contests" in which dogs, chickens, and flowers were judged and gawked at by museum visitors. But Barnum couldn't persuade respectable girls and women to take part in such an "improper" activity.

To overcome this reluctance, he hit on the idea of inviting women to submit their photographs instead, promising to commission oil portraits of the top 10 entrants. He appealed to Victorian snobbery, claiming that he was trying to encourage the fine arts. In fact, he simply wanted to increase traffic to his museum. The ruse worked and women entered in droves.

Other entrepreneurs recognized a money-making idea when they saw one. By the early 1900s, all sorts of beauty contests had been established, in which babies, toddlers, teenagers, and adults were paraded in front of audiences in order to be judged on the basis of their looks. Prior to this time, such displays had been reserved for livestock.

The first Miss America pageant was held in Atlantic City in 1921. City officials hoped that assembling a bunch of attractive young women in bathing costumes might help them lure more tourists to the seaside resort after Labor Day weekend.

By the early part of the 20th century, social views had softened, and many young women entered the competitions believing that if they won, the profile they gained would change their lives for the better. At the time, very few girls expected to go on to university—unless it was to obtain an eligible husband. If they had to work, their choices were typically limited to the designated female professions of store clerk, secretary, teacher, or nurse. You can understand the appeal of the beauty pageant: it had the potential to open the door to more opportunities. These were neither numerous nor guaranteed, but they could net a beauty queen some modeling or acting work, which tended to be more glamorous and better paying—if ultimately short-lived—than the alternatives.

Some pageant winners, then and since, have indeed gone on to greater things. After Vanessa Williams became the first African American to win the crown in 1984, she established a successful acting and singing career. Others have managed to overcome the beautiful-but-dumb stereotype that sometimes sticks to contestants to become respected TV journalists or business executives.

The stepping-stone possibilities are part of the appeal of beauty pageants even today. And they help to explain why the contests are more popular in rural areas than they are in big cities. For good-looking girls from smaller towns, where career possibilities may be more limited than they are in urban centers, beauty pageants still seem to promise a wealth of opportunity.

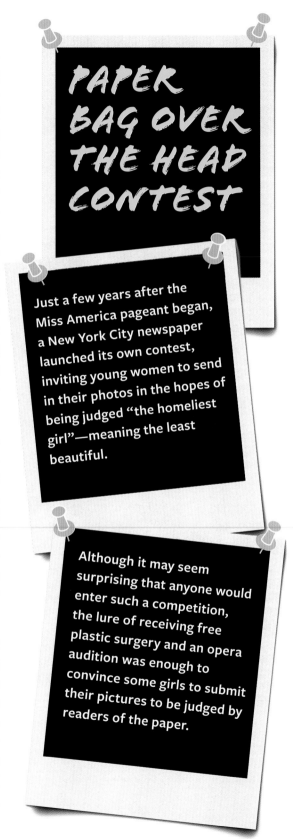

PAPER BAG OVER THE HEAD CONTEST

Just a few years after the Miss America pageant began, a New York City newspaper launched its own contest, inviting young women to send in their photos in the hopes of being judged "the homeliest girl"—meaning the least beautiful.

Although it may seem surprising that anyone would enter such a competition, the lure of receiving free plastic surgery and an opera audition was enough to convince some girls to submit their pictures to be judged by readers of the paper.

SHOULD BEAUTY PAGEANTS STILL EXIST?

"Sure, they're fine."

Beauty pageants give girls and women opportunities, and teach them confidence and poise. They celebrate women who work hard to look good and take care of themselves. We live in a society that values beauty, so if you're born with good looks, why not take advantage of it?

Many pageants aren't just about looks: contestants are also judged on personality, talent, and the poise and intelligence they demonstrate in interviews. Winners are often involved in charity work for worthy causes.

Pageants are wholesome environments for young women, rewarding good values as well as good looks. Especially compared with industries like modeling, where girls can be exploited.

For children, entering pageants is a fun activity, no more harmful than being involved in sports or music. Kids in pageants get to travel, make friends, and learn to be good winners and losers.

Little girls in pageants enjoy wearing fancy dresses and makeup—it's like playing dress-up.

Winning pageants is a chance for girls and young women to earn prize money, scholarships, and/or bonds that can give them more opportunities in life.

"No, they're harmful."

Pageants reinforce for girls and women the already pervasive message that the way they look is the most important thing about them, and that it's okay to judge women by their appearance. They present a narrow beauty ideal that's impossible for most to achieve without extreme dieting, exercise, or plastic surgery.

If pageants want to reward women for their personalities or talents, why make them parade around in bikinis and high heels, too? Judging women this way is degrading and sexist.

Pageant organizers try to dictate how contest winners should behave, and many promote a virginal ideal, disqualifying women who are married or have children. Around the world, pageant judges and organizers have been accused of corruption and accepting bribes, as well as harassment and sexual assault of candidates.

Some kids are pressured into pageant involvement by their families, and stuffed with sugar and caffeine to keep their energy up through the long hours. Children aren't equipped to deal with rejection based on how they look, and may develop emotional problems.

Child beauty pageants sexualize young girls: many undergo extensive grooming procedures, (spray tanning, waxing, fake eyelashes and nails, hair extensions), and are made to wear high heels and inappropriate outfits.

Entering pageants can cost contestants and their families thousands of dollars for dresses, grooming, traveling, entry fees, and lessons.

MISS AMERICA: BEFORE AND AFTER

Even Miss America can't always live up to her own image. Two months after being crowned the 2013 winner, Mallory Hagan was photographed on a beach looking noticeably curvier than at the time of the pageant (though still slim and healthy by almost any standards). Tabloids and internet commenters scolded her for gaining weight and "letting herself go."

But Hagan told critics to give her a break, saying that her pageant body was the result of a rigorous diet and exercise program that couldn't be maintained indefinitely—similar to preparing for a boxing match. "We get in shape and then life goes back to normal," she said in a talk show appearance. "Some days you want to eat potatoes."

CHALLENGES TO THE "Cattle Show"

Despite the popularity of pageants, and the fantasies they feed in young girls who dream of being crowned the fairest of them all, beauty contests have continued to attract controversy over the years.

In 1968, a couple of busloads of women showed up at the Miss America pageant to protest the competition. They wanted people to question the practice of judging women and girls on the basis of their physical appearance, like animals at a county fair.

The protesters crowned a live sheep and held up a poster featuring a naked woman whose body parts had been labeled "rump" and "loin" as if she were a side of beef. The publicity stunt challenged the way many people looked at the treatment of women generally, and at beauty pageants in particular.

In the years following the protest, perspectives on the rights and roles of women continued to shift, and different career

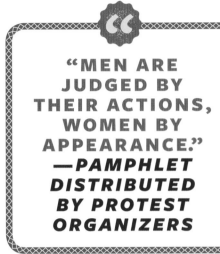

opportunities continued to open up for girls. As a result, beauty pageants began to lose some of the prominence they'd once had. Then advertising, music videos, and reality TV shows made beautiful, sexy young women more visible, and televised beauty pageants became even less of an audience draw.

But as long as the world rewards young women for living up to certain beauty ideals, there's money to be made from holding contests that judge one girl to be prettier than all the rest. Ratings for the Miss America and Miss USA telecasts have bounced back in recent years, after organizers modernized the pageants by getting TV viewers to vote on finalists by phone or text, and having winners connect with fans through social media. And reality shows like *Toddlers & Tiaras*, which focus on families who enter their little girls into child beauty pageants, have drawn increased attention—both positive and negative—to these kinds of contests.

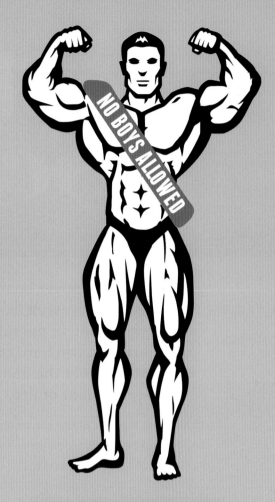

Beauty pageant contestants are almost always women and girls. Bodybuilder contests are an exception, but by their nature they attract less media attention. Arnold Schwarzenegger, who won the Mr. Universe title five times and the Mr. Olympus title seven, is world-famous today, but more because of his subsequent career as a Hollywood action hero and a politician than because of his "beauty" crowns.

This is not to say that men aren't expected to compete with each other, just that their contests have typically been played out in the realm of sports, business, or politics—where they're judged on the basis of what they know or can do, as opposed to simply how they look.

CRUEL
School

Even if you've never been remotely interested in strutting around in pursuit of a tiara, it's still hard to completely avoid the daily beauty pageant of life.

High school is often where the toughest judging takes place. Many kids feel as if their looks are being critiqued every time they walk down the halls. And sometimes they're right. A lot of teens mark each other as cool or not based on everything from facial features and body shape to clothes, makeup, and hairstyle. Such judgments can have a huge impact on not just who's popular, but on who gets ridiculed, harassed, or simply ignored. In some cases, the social stigma of not fitting in or being judged a geek is so severe that kids change schools just to escape the way they've been labeled.

And those judgments don't stop when you're off school property. For kids who use Facebook, Instagram, or other social media sites, their phones and computers can become like a virtual school hallway where classmates critique their looks and clothes. Since these locales are well out of sight of any school officials, the comments can be even nastier than they are in person.

It's not exactly the kind of problem that's easy to report. And even the knowledge that kids who put others down invariably do so out of their own feelings of insecurity doesn't change the pain of the experience.

In an effort to even the playing field on the clothing front, and to minimize distinctions between students with lots of disposable cash and students without, some public schools have introduced uniforms. The theory is that if everybody's dressed the same, nobody gets judged on where they bought their jeans or whose logo is splashed across their T-shirt.

It's not that simple, of course. Kids just come up with different means of distinguishing themselves—hem lengths, jewelry, tattoos... The criteria may change, but the feeling of having to compete often remains the same.

The
UN-WINNABLE MEDIA MATCH

◇◇◇◇◇◇◇◇◇◇◇◇◇◇◇◇◇◇◇

Beyond the schoolyard in the wider world, the stakes seem just as high, or higher.

The beautiful people who populate movies, advertisements, fashion spreads, and TV shows set an impossibly unrealistic standard against which we all feel measured.

This is particularly true for women and girls. Just think about the most visible female characters on television and in Hollywood movies: they are, almost without exception, both slim and shapely. And the female models in magazines and ads have unbelievable (literally!) bodies that don't occur very often in nature.

The popular entertainment media feature good-looking guys, too, but TV shows and films also typically have more roles for male characters who are merely average in appearance. Also, guys' bodies are not on display nearly as often as women's bodies are.

CHILL-OUT STRATEGY

People who get petty and competitive over beauty issues are probably more likely to worry about being laughed at or criticized themselves. It's like the expression, "Live by the sword, die by the sword." If you put others down for their fashion missteps or bodily faults, you invite the same kind of treatment.

Next time you find yourself mentally evaluating someone else's appearance, try focusing on only what you find appealing—the color of their shirt, their smile, or the confidence of their walk, the cut of their hair... Avoiding a critical mindset around others also makes it less likely that you'll be hard on yourself.

How does this affect the way viewers feel about their own appearance? In a word, badly. Researchers have studied the issue, and here's what they've found:

 Women and girls become less satisfied with themselves, and more critical of their appearance, when they're exposed to unrealistically thin and beautiful models and actors.

 The more time women and girls spend watching TV shows and reading magazines, the more likely they are to be negatively affected, and to become obsessed about their appearance or to develop an eating disorder.

 Male viewers were more critical of the appearance of average-looking females after looking at pictures of beautiful models. In extreme cases, guys can get so used to seeing images of unnaturally sleek women that they have difficulty forming relationships with real women.

With girls' and women's career opportunities expanding enormously in recent decades, media images have become increasingly unrealistic on the success front as well. The unconscious message is, "Sure, you can be a medical examiner, astronaut, or judge, but you'd better be skinny and beautiful, too."

COMPARISON *TECHNOLOGY*

◇◇◇◇◇◇◇◇◇◇◇◇◇◇◇◇◇◇

In this age of mass media, where we're surrounded by images of other people all the time, it's almost impossible to imagine living a few centuries ago, when the only faces and bodies we would be really familiar with would be those of our relatives and neighbors, people who lived nearby and interacted with us on a regular basis. Without the constant comparisons provided by the media—or even mirrors—we'd still notice who was good-looking and who wasn't, but we probably wouldn't think about it nearly as much.

When photography was first invented and people saw their images on film for the first time, many were unhappy with the result, and some even requested changes! Not used to seeing themselves captured in print, they found the experience very jarring.

Photography started to change how individuals thought and felt about their looks, but then mass media—magazines, film, and television—had an even bigger impact on people's sense of themselves. Suddenly, the number of people they knew and saw regularly expanded exponentially to include all sorts of people they would never, ever meet, but whose appearances became familiar and widely discussed.

With each new technological advance, the beauty stakes get higher for everybody. Being thought good-looking within our family or neighborhood isn't nearly as impressive anymore. Consciously or unconsciously, we're all now being compared to celebrities who, in addition to having won the gene lottery in the first place, are attended to by stylists, hair and makeup artists, and personal trainers.

As if that isn't difficult enough to compete with, the images of beautiful people pouring out of the entertainment industry are becoming further and further removed from reality. Special lighting, airbrushing, and computer graphics programs have all helped to create pictures of people that bear less and less resemblance to the reflections in their own mirrors.

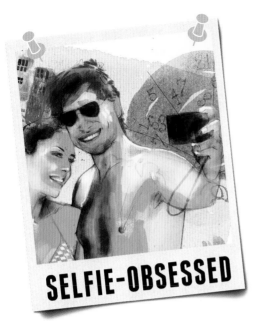

SELFIE-OBSESSED

When the general public started using the internet, in the 1990s, it seemed to offer a new kind of environment where people could be free from the baggage of their external appearances.

For anyone who didn't quite fit in in "real" life, it promised a sort of liberation: on the internet, you could chat, share things, or play games with other people, and nobody needed to know if you were overweight, acne-scarred, or unfashionably dressed.

It hasn't quite turned out that way, of course. Vast sections of the internet are devoted to sharing comments about people's perceived attractiveness—or lack of it—that most of us would never make in real life. And as the web has become more and more centered around social media, it's become harder to disconnect your online identity from your real one.

Social media sites, for instance, can be great for communicating and sharing, but they can also become a forum for obsessive and competitive feelings about looks. Some of us spend hours taking and uploading photos of ourselves to share with everyone we know, then waiting for likes, favorites, and comments, which act as a kind of referendum on how people see us. When lots of your friends like that selfie you took wearing your new T-shirt, it can feel great. But when nobody responds it can be a discouraging reminder of how easy it is to become attached to—and undermined by—some aspect of our culture's relentless beauty contest.

"FACEBOOK IS MAKING IT EASIER FOR PEOPLE TO SPEND MORE TIME AND ENERGY CRITICIZING THEIR OWN BODIES AND WISHING THEY LOOKED LIKE SOMEONE ELSE."
—DR. HARRY BRANDT, DIRECTOR OF THE CENTER FOR EATING DISORDERS

Looking at other people's images of themselves can also create feelings of unhappiness: a survey of Facebook users between 16 and 40 years old found that over half felt more conscious of their weight after looking at the site, and nearly a third said they felt sad when comparing their own photos to those of their friends. Many reported looking at photos of friends and envying their bodies. And nearly half of respondents said that when they are out at parties or other social events, they are always conscious that someone might take their picture and post it online.

Feelings of insecurity existed before the internet, of course. But as technology becomes an ever more constant part of our lives, it's getting harder to switch off the things that can trigger beauty worries and comparisons.

LIGHTS! CAMERAS! BOTOX!

The invention of high-definition television, IMAX movie screens, and powerful digital SLR cameras have introduced a new level of close-ups that not everybody's ready for. The exceptionally clear images produced by such new technologies expose the kind of skin flaws that makeup used to be able to conceal.

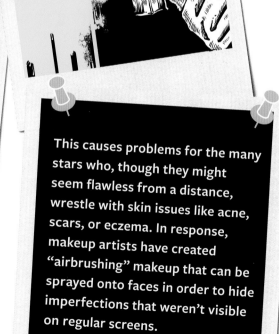

This causes problems for the many stars who, though they might seem flawless from a distance, wrestle with skin issues like acne, scars, or eczema. In response, makeup artists have created "airbrushing" makeup that can be sprayed onto faces in order to hide imperfections that weren't visible on regular screens.

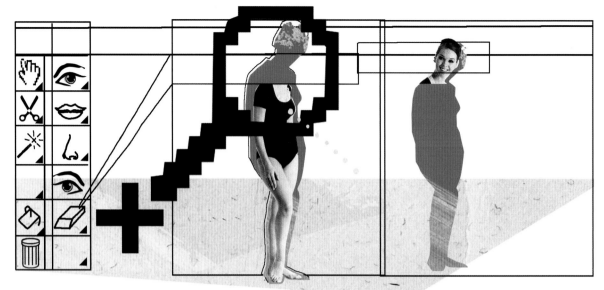

Unnatural
BEAUTY SECRETS

Most fashion photographs are retouched these days, and not just to remove the odd pimple, unflattering shadow, or wrinkle.

Modern technology allows art directors to do practically anything, from trimming a model's waist and enlarging her breasts, to changing the contours of her face or the color of her skin, to altering the color of her clothing or removing it altogether. (Try googling "Photoshop before and after" for some particularly shocking examples.) In their zeal to perfect already-stunning celebrities and models, photo editors have even accidentally removed limbs, made bodies contort in humanly impossible ways, or produced bizarre indentations in legs and

hips. Occasionally the heads of movie and sports stars are digitally placed on entirely different bodies!

Despite the reputation that models and performers have for undergoing all sorts of procedures in order to look their best, some feel that the alteration trends have gone too far. Celebrities including Beyoncé, Keira Knightley, and Kate Winslet have spoken out when photos of them were doctored to change the way their bodies really look. Others, like Jessica Simpson and Brad Pitt, have even asked to pose for magazines without any makeup, hairstyling, or photo enhancement, as a way of making a statement that even movie-star faces and bodies have wrinkles and flaws.

Many ordinary people are fed up with the excessive digital alteration of photos, too. In 2012, 14-year-old Julia Bluhm led a campaign to get fashion magazines aimed at teen girls to stop using Photoshop. She collected tens of thousands of signatures for an online petition and delivered it to the offices of *Seventeen*. The magazine's editors partially gave in, signing an agreement not to change models' sizes or shapes (though they still use it to remove things like blemishes or wrinkles in clothing). Inspired by Bluhm's success, two other girls tried the same approach with *Teen Vogue*. The editors, however, refused to meet any of their requests.

Photoshop isn't the only problem. Even without it, there's no question that magazines and ads tend to feature a narrow spectrum of human beings who are, for the most part, already exceptionally beautiful and thin. Digital alteration of their faces and bodies just takes the standards of perfection from "improbable" to "completely impossible."

Measuring Up to Barbie

The average American woman is 5'4" tall and weighs 166 pounds.

The average female model is 5'9" tall and weighs 110 pounds.

If Barbie—as in the doll— were a full-sized human being, she'd be 6'0" tall and weigh 100 pounds, and her measurements would be 39–21–33. She'd have to have all her clothes custom made and her proportions would make it hard to walk upright.

Model BEHAVIOR?

◇◇◇◇◇◇◇◇◇◇◇◇◇◇◇◇◇◇

Most girls have a better chance of winning a lottery than becoming a top model.

Bobbi Brown, a makeup artist who has her own successful line of cosmetics, provides some sobering context for how tough the competition is: "For every one hundred girls who step foot into the major American modeling agencies, only one will actually get signed by them. Even then, her chances of making it are slim… Approximately only one model in ten thousand will be able to make it her career."

The tall, slim physique prominent on catwalks and in fashion ads is something very few women or men are born with, and almost nobody can maintain indefinitely. To do so often requires chronic dieting and exercise, and sometimes more extreme tactics that can have serious health consequences. Fashion industry insiders tell stories about how models react to the enormous pressure to be thin: some starve themselves to the point where they can barely stand or open their eyes. Some eat wads of tissue paper to fill their stomachs and reduce hunger pangs. Some even go

on IV drips—which supply nutrients and a feeling of fullness without food—to drop weight quickly before a fitting or runway show.

Athletes have a bit more leeway on the body-image front. But don't forget that they spend a big part of most days working out—with the help of personal trainers or coaches—in order to maintain their edge.

DOUBLE
Take

It's hard to completely escape the pressure to compare, compete, or conform to the ideals of beauty being promoted all around you—especially if the fashion police seem to have taken over your school. But only you get to decide how much of a priority it's going to be in your life.

There's nothing wrong with making the most of the physical appearance your genes have handed you. But studies show that girls who value other things about themselves— their intelligence, athleticism, ability to play a musical instrument, close relationships with friends— aren't nearly as affected by impossible media ideals.

Time spent *doing* means less time *comparing*—and that translates into more confidence.

Beauty resentment can infect friendships and erode self-esteem. The only people who win when appearance rivalry gets ramped up are the ones profiting from fashion and makeup sales.

When looking at images of models and celebrities, keep in mind that looking gorgeous is literally *their job,* and they usually have lots of people (including Photoshop wizards) helping them to create the illusion.

FLOGGING
Fantasies

◇◇◇◇◇◇◇◇◇◇◇◇

THE DRUGSTORE ON THE CORNER
has hundreds of cosmetics, all promising to completely transform your skin, hair, and nails. The magazine rack offers "659 new ways to look cute" and "263 perfect makeup tips." And ads on your computer invite you to click for "1 tip to a flat tummy" and "8 secrets to clearer skin."

◇◇◇◇◇◇◇◇◇◇◇◇◇◇◇◇

From the salon down the street to huge international cosmetics companies, there's a lot of money to be made from our fantasies of looking better. The challenge is in wading through all the products and services on offer and figuring out which—if any—might address your concerns about your appearance. (In the process, you might reflect on what inspired you to have concerns in the first place.)

TODAY'S *MULTI-BILLION-DOLLAR BEAUTY INDUSTRY* THRIVES ON MAKING YOU FEEL THAT THERE'S ALWAYS SOMETHING TO IMPROVE ABOUT YOUR LOOKS.

BANNING BEAUTY DEVIOUSNESS

Toward the end of the 18th century, members of the British Parliament attempted to pass a law preventing women from "trapping" men with artificial means. The politicians (all male, at the time) were concerned that devious women could so effectively disguise their physical flaws with makeup and other artifices that poor, unsuspecting men would be tricked into marrying them under false pretences.

The proposed law never passed, though, because they couldn't figure out a way to enforce it.

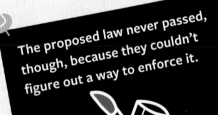

MAKE *UP*
MAKE *OVER*

◇◇◇◇◇◇◇◇◇◇◇◇◇◇◇◇◇◇◇◇

Makeup of one kind or another has been around for centuries, but it's gone in and out of style many times. During some periods, it was seen as an essential component of every fashionable woman's (and occasionally man's) beauty regimen. At other times, it was so negatively associated with actors and prostitutes (professions that were sometimes viewed as being interchangeable) that no "respectable" woman would touch it.

Even as recently as a hundred years ago, most North American women wouldn't have dreamed of wearing makeup, and beauty contestants were absolutely forbidden to do so.

But during the 1800s, some savvy businesspeople began to recognize the money-making opportunities in manufacturing and selling beauty aids. They set up companies to not only make personal products, but to convince people that they really couldn't live without them.

BEAUTY BY THE NUMBERS

How much do Americans spend on beauty per year? (2012 figures)

COSMETIC PRODUCTS: $60 BILLION

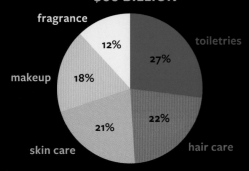

- fragrance 12%
- toiletries 27%
- makeup 18%
- hair care 22%
- skin care 21%

COSMETIC PROCEDURES: $11 BILLION

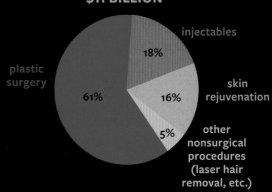

- injectables 18%
- plastic surgery 61%
- skin rejuvenation 16%
- other nonsurgical procedures (laser hair removal, etc.) 5%

$61 billion

Weight-loss products and services

$2.5 billion

Nail products and services

#50

Number of products sold every second by L'Oréal, the world's largest cosmetics company

$15,000

Amount the average American woman spends on makeup in her lifetime

$1.2 million/minute

Amount reportedly paid to Nicole Kidman for a 3-minute Chanel cosmetics commercial

---

How do beauty companies spend their money?

For every **$1** spent on product development

around **$10** is spent on packaging and promotion

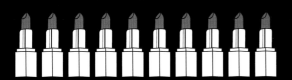

What are you paying for when you buy a bottle of $100 celebrity perfume?

- **$2** Perfume
- **$10** Bottle design and packaging
- **$8** Marketing
- **$15** Manufacturer's profit
- **$6** Salespeople's commissions
- **$15** Manufacturer's overhead
- **$25** Store's overhead
- **$4** Licensing fee for using celebrity's name
- **$15** Store's profit

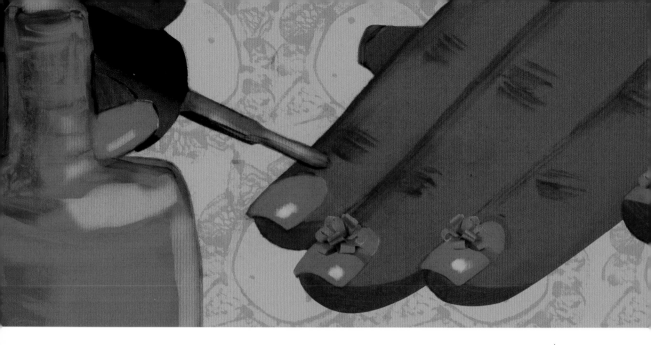

BECAUSE
You're Worth It!

◇◇◇◇◇◇◇◇◇◇◇◇◇◇◇◇◇◇◇

In a famous advertising campaign for L'Oréal, actor Cybill Shepherd—a beauty icon of the 1970s and 1980s— tossed her silky blond hair and claimed that she used the hair color because "I'm worth it!"

On one level, the slogan was a clever way to play on the traditional idea about women having a duty to make themselves gorgeous for guys. When the L'Oréal campaign was first launched in 1972, debate raged about the importance of equal rights for women. So although the company was selling beauty improvement products, its

emphasis on the woman's worth was an appealing message. The "I'm worth it" slogan told women that they were important, and deserved to do something special for themselves.

Over 40 years later, L'Oréal's advertising continues to use variations of the "I'm worth it" slogan, and its message has had a lasting cultural effect. Today many girls and women view their beauty rituals and indulgences as an empowering personal choice, rather than attempts to live up to unattainable ideals. But it's still worth asking: where did those views come from, and who benefits when women embrace them?

HOPE in a Jar

Cosmetics marketing is a highly seductive art. From commercials featuring carefully chosen celebrities, to contests and inspiring slogans on social media pages, to enticingly designed packaging, beauty brands are selling us a lot more than nail polish or moisturizer. They tell a story about who we want to be, appealing to our deepest hopes and desires—not just to be beautiful, but to be loved, special, admired. Lipstick, after all, is just colored wax in a tube. Advertising is where the real magic happens.

Judging by the success of big companies like L'Oréal, Estée Lauder, and CoverGirl, the strategy is working. We're spending more and more money every year, hoping that this moisturizer or that mascara will hide our flaws or transform us into the person we've always dreamed of being.

"IN OUR FACTORY, WE MAKE LIPSTICK; IN OUR ADVERTISING, WE SELL HOPE." — CHARLES REVSON, FOUNDER OF REVLON COSMETICS

THE natural LOOK?

If you believe some of the marketing hype around cosmetics, it's not just important to look flawless—it's also important to appear as though it required no expense or effort.

A classic ad for Clairol, for example, claimed to deliver "Hair color so natural, only her hairdresser knows for sure." Along those lines, Maybelline's famous "Maybe she's born with it" slogan implies that their mascara will make you seem naturally gifted with long, dark lashes. And cosmetics counters feature products with names like "Invisible Fluid Foundation" or "Bare Skin Makeup," with the main selling point being that nobody will know you're wearing them.

Meanwhile, beauty magazines, websites, and YouTube videos offer tutorials on how to achieve the perfect "no-makeup" look—usually with the aid of quite a bit of makeup. A typical feature from *Cosmopolitan* magazine gave the reader instructions on how to make herself up to look "natural," using 10 separate steps and 7 different makeup products!

PROMISES, PROMISES

◇◇◇◇◇◇◇◇◇◇◇◇◇◇◇◇◇◇

You can't get more than a dozen pages into the latest fashion magazine without the claims piling up:

 "Sky-high curves" for your eyelashes.

 "Dramatically whiter teeth in just two hours!"

 "Dazzling, plumping lip color."

And one shampoo ad really goes out on a limb, offering not only to transform your hair "so it's soft, silky, and full of life," but to "revitalize you," too!

How do you actually measure whether or not these products deliver? Clearly "sky-high curves" is an exaggeration you're not even expected to believe. But how does lip color "dazzle," and who's to decide whether the improved whiteness you notice after "just two hours" qualifies as "dramatic"? And what would a shampoo have to contain to actually "revitalize" you?

Such vague and meaningless phrases are invariably accompanied by pictures of fabulous-looking guys and girls who have the perfect teeth, glossy hair, or exceptional eyelashes being promised. But whether a promotional campaign features a world-famous actor or an anonymous model, the photograph is completely irrelevant to the effectiveness of the products being sold.

Pictures are powerful, but we all know that the women and men shown in the ads are chosen because they *already have* gorgeous skin or fabulous hair. And the reason they're prepared to smile into cameras is because they're being paid a lot of money to do so. Their role is similar to the salesperson at a car dealership—selling the goods is their job.

Cosmetics companies also like to pump up their advertising and packaging with scientific-sounding words and claims: this mascara delivers "80% fuller lashes" or this cream "regenerates skin at the cellular level." Scientists, however, are capable of disproving much of the hype. For instance, some dermatologists point out that adding vitamins, minerals, and herbs to many beauty products does nothing for the health of the skin or hair. Usually, the doses are too small to have any effect, or the molecules are too big to penetrate skin.

And when mixed with other ingredients or packaged improperly, they sometimes lose their effectiveness. (As just one example, vitamin A breaks down when exposed to air or light.) And it's been shown that most vitamins added to shampoos and other hair care products are useless, because hair is dead and can't absorb and metabolize nutrients the way your digestive system does.

Both Canada and the United States have regulations designed to prevent advertisers from making false claims in their promotions. And beauty companies sometimes get in trouble for ads that mislead consumers about what their products can achieve: CoverGirl, Lancôme, and Dior, for instance, have all been forced to pull mascara ads because regulators said the dramatic eyes pictured in their ads owed more to false lashes and Photoshop than to makeup.

But many of the terms and expressions used in cosmetics and beauty ads are ambiguous enough that they fall through the cracks. Beauty marketers are extremely skilled at using combinations of words and images to suggest benefits, without making direct claims that could get them in legal trouble. So as with many consumer products, a good attitude to adopt in general is "buyer beware."

Products sold only over the internet require extra caution, since they can often get around national regulations. Makeup and skin treatments bought from overseas can include ingredients that aren't

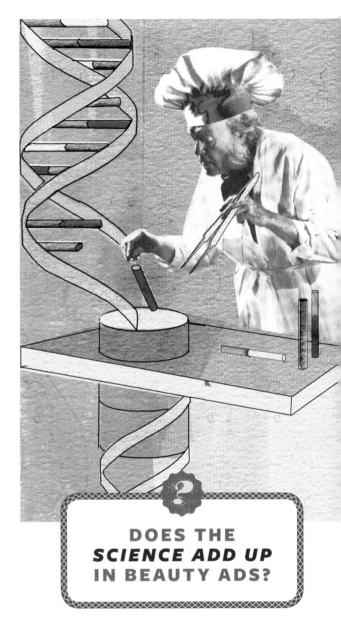

DOES THE SCIENCE ADD UP IN BEAUTY ADS?

approved for use in Canada or the US, and may be unsafe. Many people have suffered burns, for instance, from skin treatments bought over the internet that contained dangerously high concentrations of acid.

DECONSTRUCTING BEAUTY ADS

	PSEUDOSCIENCE	MISLEADING TEST RESULTS	ANGEL DUSTING
Hype			
Words to Watch For 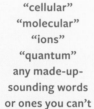	"cellular" "molecular" "ions" "quantum" any made-up-sounding words or ones you can't pronounce	"clinically proven" "dermatologist tested" "scientific results" "in vitro studies"	"with (miracle ingredient)" "enriched with" "contains"
What They Mean	These words sound technical and impressive, but are often meaningless. Beauty marketers like to confuse consumers with talk about the scientific properties of substances, without saying how (or whether) they make you look better when you rub them on your skin.	Ask yourself: what tests were conducted? On how many people? Under what conditions? What were they compared to? Companies almost never release full details about their testing, and usually conduct the tests themselves, so what these claims actually mean is anyone's guess.	Say an ingredient—let's call it Snaxiol—is all over the news because it's been shown to make skin smoother. But Snaxiol is expensive, and only effective if used in high concentrations. If you were running a cosmetics company, you might decide to put a trace amount of Snaxiol in your skin cream—not enough to cost you very much, of course (or to be effective). Then, in your advertising, you could claim the cream "contains Snaxiol, proven to keep skin smooth." You'd benefit from the good press about Snaxiol, without having to say how it actually works in your product. This practice is called "angel dusting" and it's common—and perfectly legal—in the cosmetics world.

Beauty marketing is carefully designed to bypass your rational mind, but once you learn some of the tricks of the trade, you can start to see through the hype. Notice which phrases or images suck you in, and then look at each word individually. Here are some typical puff strategies to watch for.

GREENWASHING

"natural"
"pure"
"organic ingredients"
"eco"
"green"

Many consumers seek out "natural" products believing they're safer and better. But lots of "natural" substances aren't remotely healthy—poison ivy is natural, and lead might be pure, but you wouldn't want either one anywhere near your face! Meanwhile, some synthetic ingredients are perfectly safe, and even beneficial. "Green" terms aren't regulated by the government, so a product marked "natural" could contain two or three natural ingredients, along with a dozen synthetic chemicals.

MISLEADING ANIMAL TESTING CLAIMS

"cruelty-free"
"not tested on animals"
"against animal testing"

Do these statements mean that no animals were hurt in the making of your foundation or mascara? Not necessarily. Brands can commission outside suppliers or labs to test individual ingredients on animals, but as long as the company itself doesn't conduct animal tests on the final product, they can claim to be "cruelty-free." If the issue matters to you, look for a third-party logo (such as Leaping Bunny) certifying that no animal testing has been done at any step of production.

WRIGGLE WORDS

"may"
"seem"
"appear"
"virtually"
"helps"
"rejuvenating"
"stimulating"

These words are deliberately vague. Beware of claims such as "makes dark circles seem to disappear" or "helps the appearance of wrinkles." Meanwhile, words like "rejuvenating" and "stimulating" sound impressive and evoke good feelings, but don't mean anything specific. They seem to promise great things to consumers eager to improve a tired appearance, but are vague enough to avoid saying what they actually do to your skin or hair.

IT'S NOT JUST THE
Miracle Bra

◇◇◇◇◇◇◇◇◇◇◇◇◇◇◇

When one newspaper journalist went behind the scenes at a photo shoot for a lingerie advertising campaign, she discovered some tricks of the trade used both during the shoot and in photo editing afterwards.

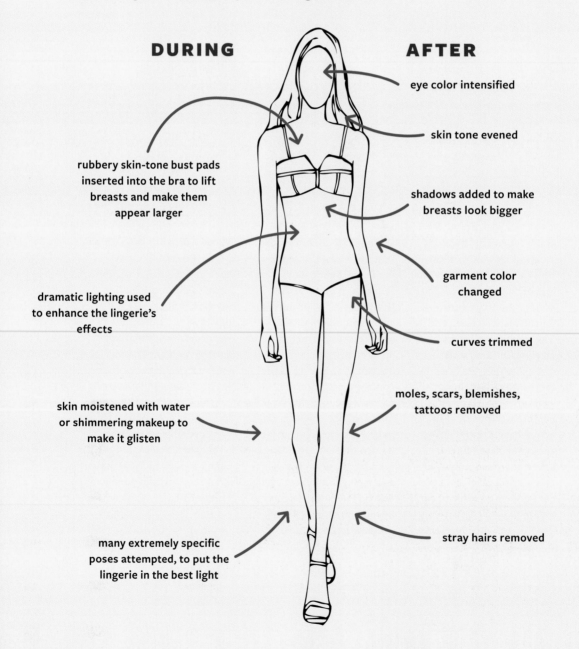

DURING

AFTER

eye color intensified

skin tone evened

rubbery skin-tone bust pads inserted into the bra to lift breasts and make them appear larger

shadows added to make breasts look bigger

garment color changed

dramatic lighting used to enhance the lingerie's effects

curves trimmed

moles, scars, blemishes, tattoos removed

skin moistened with water or shimmering makeup to make it glisten

stray hairs removed

many extremely specific poses attempted, to put the lingerie in the best light

Made Up OR *Au Naturel?*

Lots of women (and some guys) wear makeup. Many other women prefer not to. Some won't be seen without it, while others just wear it for special occasions. Some like subtle enhancements, and others view their faces as canvases for bold color and artistic expression. People's views on makeup are as individual as they are, and judging its effects on someone's appearance can be highly subjective. What are the arguments for and against it?

PRO

Makeup is creative and fun, and lets you express yourself and experiment with different looks.

Makeup evens the playing field: it lets you emphasize your good features and downplay flaws. It allows women to cover up scarring or skin conditions they might feel self-conscious about.

Makeup brings people pleasure: a pretty lipstick or colorful eyeliner can brighten your day. It's about doing something just for yourself.

Most girls and women don't feel obligated to wear lots of makeup, or to wear it all the time—it's freedom of choice.

A number of cosmetics brands contain natural ingredients and don't test on animals. Certain ones even donate a percentage of their profits to good causes.

CON

Makeup covers your natural skin and features, disguising your true self.

Because so many women wear makeup, women who choose not to are the ones who stand out. Women's natural faces can start to seem like the exception if we're more used to seeing cosmetically enhanced ones.

The persistent double standard means women are expected to spend time and money on makeup and men aren't.

Some women feel uncomfortable even going to the gym or grocery store without makeup. Because of the societal pressure to look a certain way, the choice is not truly free.

Producing makeup and packaging has an impact on the environment. Also, many cosmetics contain ingredients that can be harmful to your health, and most major cosmetics brands are tested on animals.

DO YOU GET WHAT YOU PAY FOR?

Many people assume that expensive beauty products must work better than cheap ones. Yet pricey skin creams and lipsticks are often similar to less expensive ones—they just usually have nicer packaging. Most beauty experts agree there are good and bad products at all points on the price spectrum.

As Perry Romanowski, a cosmetic chemist, has put it, "Some skin-care products... cost about $2 to make, but then are on sale for $300. Other skin-care products can be made for 50 cents and are sold for $2." So-called "luxury" brands will always charge more—not necessarily because they contain rare and exotic ingredients, but to maintain their high-end status.

FEATURED *Puff*

◇◇◇◇◇◇◇◇◇◇◇◇◇◇◇◇◇◇◇

You have to read between the lines in magazine and web articles as well as in ads.

Most magazines and websites wouldn't exist without the money that companies pay them for advertising space. As a result, some mags offer advertisers special bonuses in the form of photo features and sidebars that are really advertisements disguised as objective information. Recognizing that readers are more likely to believe the claims made in an article than an ad, advertisers often demand both. They pay for a full-page ad, but also expect the writers to mention their products in the editorial sections, and include links to their website or list locations where the items can be purchased. Or they pay for "advertorials" or "sponsored content," which are designed to look like an article or interview so readers won't notice they're actually ads.

This means there's less emphasis on home remedies—like the use of sliced cucumber or used tea bags to reduce puffy eyes—than on store-bought treatments. The fashion spread's models will be made up with products advertised elsewhere in the magazine, and the seemingly random list of hot new products being recommended by the beauty editors will feature items promoted in paid ads. And you won't see many articles in women's magazines that criticize beauty practices featured in ads elsewhere in the magazine. The people running the publications are careful to avoid printing stories that might upset the advertisers who support them.

So try this: next time you read an over-the-top endorsement of some new cleanser or notice that a makeover features a lot of a particular makeup line, flip through the pages of the magazine, or look along the edges of the web page. The chances are high that you'll discover ads for those particular products or companies.

The Credibility Diet

Here's a skill-testing question: the cover of a magazine promises you details of a new diet that will allow you to lose 10 pounds in 10 days so you can fit into those jeans you grew out of two years ago. Do you spend five bucks on the magazine, or save up to buy a new pair of jeans that actually fit?

Weight-loss schemes—including diets, pills, supplements, creams, and special programs—are among the biggest scams in the beauty business. Despite years of evidence proving that very few of them work, the companies selling promises of slimness continue to make millions.

Most of us know better than to believe that we'll lose five pounds a week eating all the protein bars we want, or drop three dress sizes in a month by starting every day with grapefruit. Websites, magazines, and advertisers making these promises are just counting on making money from our ignorance and gullibility. They succeed because of the stigma North American culture attaches to being overweight. And the more attention the media give to weight and dieting, the bigger the stigma becomes.

But here's the scary part: for many people, the more they diet, the fatter they get. The US Federal Trade Commission has estimated that only five percent of the millions of Americans who go on a slimming diet each year will succeed in losing weight and keeping it off. One study found that people who went on diets actually gained *more* weight over a two-year period than non-dieters.

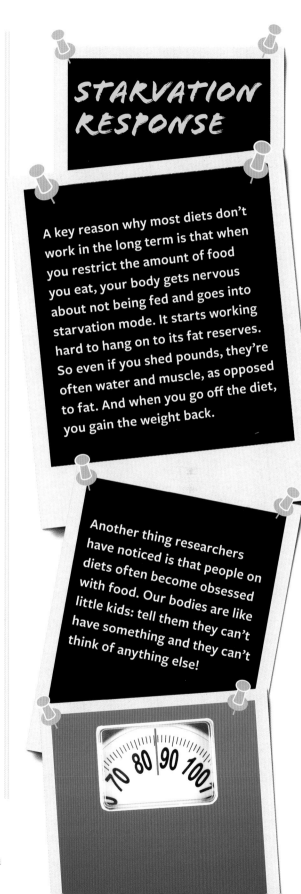

STARVATION RESPONSE

A key reason why most diets don't work in the long term is that when you restrict the amount of food you eat, your body gets nervous about not being fed and goes into starvation mode. It starts working hard to hang on to its fat reserves. So even if you shed pounds, they're often water and muscle, as opposed to fat. And when you go off the diet, you gain the weight back.

Another thing researchers have noticed is that people on diets often become obsessed with food. Our bodies are like little kids: tell them they can't have something and they can't think of anything else!

WHEN THE REMEDY'S
More Dangerous
THAN THE DISEASE

◇◇◇◇◇◇◇◇◇◇◇◇◇◇◇◇◇◇◇◇

If you wanted to lose 20 pounds, would you willingly trade them for heart problems, insomnia, or drug addiction? Lots of people have, without realizing that was the deal. Diet pills and weight-loss supplements are often made to sound like salvation in a bottle and the information provided in promotional materials tends to downplay the possible side effects. But as a result of serious medical problems and even a number of deaths, many diet drugs and herbal weight-loss supplements have been banned, and new ones are pulled off the market due to safety concerns every year. In addition, the US Food and Drug Administration and Health Canada regularly issue warnings about unsafe diet pills sold online.

As with cosmetics advertising, it's handy to be skeptical when considering the claims made by suppliers of diet products or programs. Beware of medical-sounding jargon, of "secret formulas" or anonymous studies. Watch out for personal testimonials, too. Even if the thinner, happier people featured in an ad's "after" photos aren't celebrities, chances are they've been paid to tell "their story," and to imply that what worked for them will work for you. Online product reviews, likewise, may be paid for by the weight-loss companies that make them.

Comprehensive weight-loss plans certainly help some people, but they, too, have their critics. Undercover journalists posing as potential clients have reported that some programs use high-pressure sales tactics, fail to consider individuals' unique medical needs, and deliberately confuse clients with complicated pricing systems. People may sign up for a program and realize partway through that the promised results are only "guaranteed" if they buy thousands of dollars' worth of special food or supplements. Others feel so defeated when they are unable to lose the weight that they blame themselves, or are too embarrassed about being ripped off to lodge a complaint.

> **WEIGHT-LOSS PROMISES THAT SOUND TOO GOOD TO BE TRUE *USUALLY ARE.***

Independent experts—such as doctors and nutritionists who aren't making money from weight-loss schemes—tend to agree: any plan that promises fast weight loss and recommends something other than a balanced approach to nutrition and regular exercise is likely to be a fraudulent fad.

The same principles hold true for products promoted in gyms and sold in sports stores, that promise weight gain. Few, if any, of them produce the kind of results shown in magazine ads. Some bodies are simply designed to build up muscles more easily than others, and the ads feature guys who not only have the right physique, but also must invest countless hours in the gym, not just rely on health formulas to keep them fit. Then comes the Photoshopping!

DON'T SMILE FOR THE CAMERA

Not everyone in Hollywood salutes the trend toward messing around with nature. Acclaimed movie directors like Martin Scorsese and Baz Luhrmann, along with many casting directors and studio executives, are critical of the way in which plastic surgery techniques can seriously limit a face's expressiveness. They complain that stars who attempt to recapture a more youthful look through face-lifts, Botox injections, or fillers have lost the ability to communicate grief or joy. Says Luhrmann, "Their faces can't really move properly."

In fact, some actors who have these procedures done in an effort to get more work find the strategy ends up backfiring. No one will hire them because of their strangely frozen foreheads and swollen lips—unless it's to play characters who have had too much plastic surgery.

"SHE GOT HER LOOKS FROM HER FATHER. HE'S A PLASTIC SURGEON."
—COMEDIAN GROUCHO MARX

MAKE ME *OVER*

◇◇◇◇◇◇◇◇◇◇◇◇◇◇◇◇◇◇

Beauty makeovers have been a staple of women's magazines for decades.

Readers have always been fascinated by the kind of real-life Cinderella stories that makeovers represent. We get vicarious satisfaction out of watching a person being transformed from a caterpillar into a butterfly. And seeing becomes believing: if they did it, we think, so can we. We fantasize about what it would be like to eliminate our own imperfections.

In the 21st century, reality television pushed the makeover phenomenon to a whole new level. Where magazines and daytime talk shows changed people's hairstyles, makeup, and clothing, TV shows like *Extreme Makeover* and *The Swan* offered much more invasive procedures, like orthodontic work, face-lifts, and breast implants. Later, the extreme-makeover trend seeped offscreen, with young female reality stars tweeting photos of their implants and tummy tucks, and having their pre- and post-surgery bodies exhaustively scrutinized in the media.

People who undergo these highly public makeovers often do seem transformed. For some, an updated hairstyle and flattering clothes are enough to make them seem younger, thinner, and more confident and attractive. Others, whose self-consciousness about a large nose or bad teeth severely restricted their lives, say in interviews that cosmetic surgery helped them feel "normal" and "free." Many report being happier, socializing more, or getting better job opportunities. Some say they feel their exterior finally matches the person they always were inside. Clinton Kelly, who

UNREALITY STAR

Heidi Montag, who appeared on the reality show *The Hills*, has become a poster girl for the downsides of excessive plastic surgery. At age 23, she had 10 procedures in one day—including breast implants, liposuction, and work on her ears, chin, neck, legs, and lower back. When she was filmed going home after the bandages came off, her family reacted with shock: rather than congratulating her on her new Barbie-style look, her mother just said sadly that she thought she was more beautiful before.

Montag later said she regretted the surgeries, which caused her extreme pain, left scars all over her body, and nearly broke up her marriage. "I almost risked everything, all my relationships, and myself, for vanity," she told a TV news program. "Sometimes I wish I could just go back to the original Heidi."

co-hosted the makeover program *What Not to Wear*, commented that his show was at its essence "about taking stock of who you are and communicating that non-verbally to the rest of the world."

In some cases, however, makeover subjects have so much work done, they emerge looking like completely different people. And the reactions of those closest to them can be upsetting. For instance, when one participant on *Extreme Makeover* was first "revealed" after her transformation, her four-year-old son said, "That's not my mommy," and her stunned husband would only say that she looked "different."

If the media play a role in showing the difference that plastic surgery can make, they also play a role in creating the perceived need for it. It's a bit of a vicious circle. When we read magazines and watch television, many of the most prominent images we see of models and actors have been altered into a state of idealized perfection. We've become conditioned to see real human bodies—our own and other people's—as much less attractive in comparison.

In fact, research has found that the more exaggerated the bodies are, the more negative their impact is on viewers' self-esteem. Looking at untouched photos featuring good-looking women whose bodies haven't been surgically altered doesn't undermine women's confidence nearly as much as looking at graphically enhanced images of surgically altered or exceptionally thin models.

Maybe it's progress, of a sort, that the kinds of procedures that celebrities used to go to great lengths to hide are now more out in the open, and we can all see that the "perfect" faces and bodies in the media don't often come naturally. On the other hand, now that it's possible to alter our appearances so drastically, is there more pressure to "fix" our every flaw?

STACKING THE DECK

Those "before and after" pictures you see in makeover stories or weight-loss ads are usually carefully crafted to make transformations appear more dramatic than they really are. The "before" photos are often shot under fluorescent light or outside. The person wears casual clothes and no makeup, refrains from smiling, and often appears slumped, with unwashed hair.

In contrast, the "after" photos are taken with the aid of studio lights and colored gels, which improve skin tone. In addition to having had her hair and makeup professionally done, the makeover subject wears fancy clothes and a brilliant smile. No wonder she looks transformed!

DOUBLE
Take

As more and more North Americans choose radical means of changing their appearances, it starts to seem like a normal thing to do. Where will it stop? Will monthly injections or plastic surgery become as commonplace as regular dental checkups? If so, will Hollywood-style good looks eventually become so ordinary that we'll lose interest in beauty? Maybe our definitions of what's stunning will simply change to embrace appearances that are rare and unusual.

It's also possible that most of us will decide the physical and financial costs of these practices outweigh the benefits. In the meantime, it's good to keep honing your critical thinking skills so you can apply them to all the promises being made by the beauty industry—the explicit ones made with words, and the ones merely implied by images.

Nobody's going to put it on a billboard, so you just have to remind yourself: not even supermodels look like the images in ads and magazines! Those images are a creation of lighting, makeup, computer graphics, and sometimes surgery.

Cosmetic surgery can make a big difference to a person's appearance, but it's very expensive, often painful, requires ongoing investment, and isn't going to solve underlying emotional or psychological problems.

Many of the companies trying to separate you from your money are willing to stretch the truth in order to do so. If the claims being made sound far-fetched, they probably are.

BEYOND *Image*

YOU ARE NOT YOUR NOSE.

Or your butt, or the cold sore on your upper lip. You are not your hair—on good or bad days. You are not your legs or your lips or the mole that only you know about.

And when people look at you, they don't see you the way you see your reflection in the mirror. They're not distracted by that little voice nattering away in your head—the one telling you how much hotter you'd look if you lost 10 pounds or had clearer skin. Nine times out of ten, their inner dialogue is way more focused on whether or not *they're* measuring up than whether or not you are.

Really.

YOU ARE SO
MUCH MORE
THAN THE WAY
YOU LOOK.

Happiness
NOT GUARANTEED

◇◇◇◇◇◇◇◇◇◇◇◇◇◇◇◇◇

Most of us probably fantasize, at least once in a while, about what life would be like if the self-perceived flaws in our appearance were fixed overnight. We might imagine it would solve all our problems, or at least some of them. But even though it might seem otherwise, being beautiful has little bearing on whether or not you'll live "happily ever after."

Celebrity news websites, tabloids, and reality TV shows are full of gorgeous stars suffering from all sorts of personal problems: drug addiction, emotional breakdowns, derailed relationships, financial hardships, troubles with the law. Beauty—even when it's accompanied by fame and fortune—is no guarantee that things will always go your way.

One study on the link between beauty and happiness grouped people into categories based on how attractive others ranked them. Of the group ranked the most attractive, 55 percent said they were satisfied with their lives. For the group judged least attractive, the figure was 45 percent. Considering all the advantages that come with being hot, and all the disadvantages of being *not*, it's surprising that those people seen as more attractive are only 10 percent more likely to describe themselves as being happy.

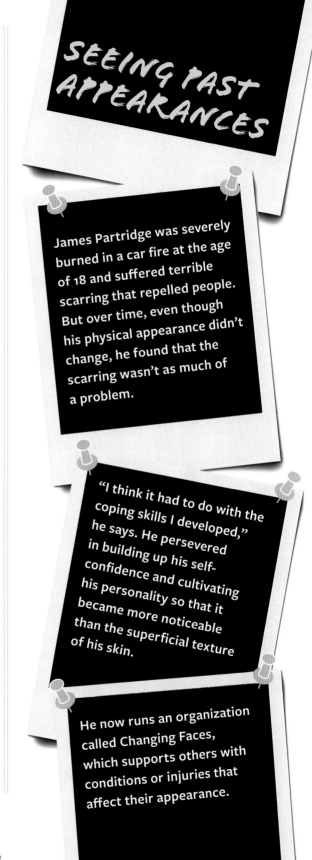

SEEING PAST APPEARANCES

James Partridge was severely burned in a car fire at the age of 18 and suffered terrible scarring that repelled people. But over time, even though his physical appearance didn't change, he found that the scarring wasn't as much of a problem.

"I think it had to do with the coping skills I developed," he says. He persevered in building up his self-confidence and cultivating his personality so that it became more noticeable than the superficial texture of his skin.

He now runs an organization called Changing Faces, which supports others with conditions or injuries that affect their appearance.

PERFORMANCE *Pressure*

Isn't it great to hang out with family or close friends, without having to worry about what you're wearing or how you look?

Well, sometimes being gorgeous—and caring about it—means you have to kiss that goodbye.

If the way people relate to you is mostly shaped by how great you look, keeping up that appearance can become a necessary chore. It's like being a basketball star or straight-A student: once you've established that you're good at something, and people expect it of you, you feel pressure to maintain the illusion that you're perfect.

For those whose careers are dependent on having a buff body or flawless face, the concern is a legitimate one: tabloids and gossip sites are full of candid photos of stars in various states of imperfection. If they go out

of the house with a baseball cap over their unwashed hair and sunglasses designed to hide the fact that they haven't slept well, chances are the paparazzi are going to snap their picture and sell it to the world. Then tabloids, websites, and TV shows assemble panels of "fashion police" to provide snarky commentary on the star's every offending thigh dimple or visible panty line. Kind of raises the stakes on having a bad hair day!

In fact, if you read enough celebrity interviews, it becomes clear that lots of stars are insecure about their looks. We might roll our eyes at the thin, beautiful movie star who claims she's "just like everyone else" because she hates her bony knees or gummy smile, but the anxieties she expresses probably sound familiar. Does that mean it's a natural part of being human, or do celebrities just hold themselves to a higher standard of perfection because of the business they're in?

MODELS SPEAK OUT

What's the modeling life *really* like? Three former models—
Morgan, Agata, and Elia (a guy)—offer some insider perspectives:

On...	Models say:
The power of modeling	"There were times when I felt very powerful because there's such a reverence in our culture for models and if you tell people you're going off to Paris for a shoot, their eyes really light up."—Agata
The benefits of the job	"Modeling gave me a huge confidence boost."—Morgan
The demands of a shoot	"You're really just a commodity. You've got the stylist, the makeup and hair people, and you're really just sitting there wondering when is this going to be over... And there are days when it takes four or five hours to take *one* picture."—Agata
Competition	"You're a piece of meat. You go to an audition and there might be 50 other beautiful people there. So you don't stand out. It's very competitive."—Elia
The pressure to stay young	"Even 24 is too old. I've had to lie about my age and say I was 21 in order to be considered for some jobs."—Morgan
Measuring up	"No matter how good you look, sometimes it's not going to be good enough for the people who are hiring."—Elia
The constant scrutiny	"It really started to chip away at my self-esteem. At one moment you would be told, 'Oh, look at these pictures, you're so beautiful,' and in the next you would be told, 'You'd be so much more beautiful if you could lose 10 more pounds.'"—Agata
Insecurity	"Models are the most insecure people on the planet. Someone is always telling you how good-looking you are, but then you get cut down for having fat legs, even though you're actually anorexic. It really messes with your mind. You look in the mirror, and you don't actually see what's really there."—Elia
Expectations from guys	"I saw lots of girls who attracted really rich boyfriends, who took them away on trips all the time, and bought them expensive presents. But there are always expectations that come with that. Nothing really comes for free—usually they want something from you in return."—Morgan
Quitting modeling	"I really felt myself dying as a person. I was constantly hungry and it became the center of my life. I was unable to derive any pleasure from being in Paris or Germany, because it was this constant obsession with being thin, with not eating. I was miserable."—Agata
Modeling as a career	"Modeling doesn't fulfill me enough as a career. It's not stimulating mentally and you don't have any personal impact through what you're doing."—Morgan

A MODEL
Profession

◇◇◇◇◇◇◇◇◇◇◇◇◇◇◇◇

In our beauty-obsessed society, the model is queen.

Just the word *model* is like a stamp certifying that you're beautiful, and therefore someone to be admired, envied, and desired. It certainly sounds like a glamorous career: jetting all over the world, posing for pictures, being fussed over by hair and makeup people, and wearing exquisite designer clothes, all while earning millions. It's no wonder so many people fantasize about doing it for a living: in a 2008 survey of teenage girls in the UK, nearly a third picked modeling as their top career choice.

Just like beauty pageants, modeling lures in pretty girls from all over the world, often from places where there are limited opportunities—strutting down a runway in Tokyo can seem like a good way to make money and escape small-town life. While plenty of models have great experiences, get to see the world, and earn good money, for others it's a mixed experience at best. The industry is rife with exploitation of inexperienced young people. And the vast majority of models don't make a ton of money. In fact, the average American model earns about $27,000 a year—less than a typical security guard or receptionist.

What are some of the realities of the job?

⬤ **Young hopefuls trying to get signed by an agency are often encouraged to take modeling courses. Some agencies are known to fatten their bank accounts by encouraging kids who don't have a chance of becoming professional to spend thousands of dollars on training.**

⬤ **Many beginning models are immediately told to lose weight, even if they're already thin. A survey done by the Model Alliance, an organization established by a group of models and fashion industry leaders to improve working conditions, found that 64 percent of respondents were asked to shed pounds by their agencies, and nearly half had done fasts, "cleanses," or gone on restrictive diets. Almost a third said they suffered from eating disorders at some point.**

⬤ **Models get to travel a lot, to exciting cities like Paris, London, New York, and Tokyo. But dragging a portfolio of photographs around**

> **"YOU NEED TO LOSE MORE WEIGHT. THE LOOK THIS YEAR IS ANOREXIC. WE DON'T WANT YOU TO *BE* ANOREXIC, WE JUST WANT YOU TO LOOK IT."**
> —*TOP MODEL COCO ROCHA, REPEATING ADVICE SHE RECEIVED AS A TEENAGER FROM PEOPLE IN THE FASHION INDUSTRY*

to a dozen auditions a day in some foreign city can be tiring, lonely, and demoralizing. So can standing for hours in front of potential clients while they critically assess every part of your body.

⬤ New models are often flown across the world and put up in apartments by their agencies, with the expectation that once they start earning money, they'll repay the costs. However, in the modeling business, you often just don't have the look they're after and there's nothing you can do about it. Some models end up owing their agencies tens of thousands of dollars, and the challenge then becomes paying them back.

⬤ While some models do earn a lot of money, many of those just starting out find their incomes are outweighed by the costs of living in big, expensive cities like New York or London, where so much modeling work is based. Magazine photo shoots usually pay $100–$400 a day—minus the agency's commission fees and taxes. Runway models are sometimes given clothes in lieu of money, which may sound great until your rent cheque is due, or you need groceries. And sometimes models are cheated out of money by unscrupulous agencies, or have to go through huge hassles just to get paid what they're owed.

⬤ One of the upsides of modeling? Fancy parties. Promoters regularly invite models out to restaurants and clubs, then buy them dinner, drinks, and sometimes drugs, and give them access to VIP areas where they get to meet famous people—all in the hope that the models' presence will attract more customers. For young models especially, the attention and privileges can be very seductive. But the perks are always accompanied by expectations, and can ultimately lead naïve newcomers into distressing situations they didn't anticipate.

⬤ Many models have spoken about being pressured by photographers to remove all their clothes, and about unwanted sexual advances or abuse. Some don't report harassment for fear of hurting their careers. The Model Alliance survey found that almost 87 percent of respondents had been asked to pose nude without being told beforehand. Nearly 30 percent experienced inappropriate touching on the job, and around the same number were pressured to have sex with someone at work. Of those, fewer than a third felt they could tell their agency, and of the ones who did complain, the majority were told by their agents that they didn't see a problem.

⬤ After a few years of modeling—if you don't go broke or starve—you're too old, and a whole new crop of younger models is coming up to replace you. All but a few top models have an expiration date, usually sometime in their 20s. Many find themselves having to start all over again in a new career, often without a college degree or any work experience outside of modeling.

beau•ty ('byoōtē)

noun (pl. beauties)

1. the combination of all the qualities of a person or thing that delight the senses and please the mind.

EXPAND THE DEFINITION

Look up "beauty" in the dictionary. It defines the word as "the combination of all the qualities of a person or thing that delight the senses and please the mind."

Combination. Not *one* single feature, but the sum total of a person's qualities, which might include intelligence, humor, generosity, and grace. Given that we only have so much control over the way we look, why not enhance our attractiveness with a little attention elsewhere?

Who you are really can alter what you look like. Research has found that beautiful people with disagreeable personalities become less attractive over time. This is partly because as we age, repeated facial expressions create lines and wrinkles. People who frequently smile and laugh end up having more attractive lines than those who scowl and carry a lot of anger. In another study, women who had been warm and outgoing as teens were judged to be better looking in their 50s than their snobby or unfriendly peers, regardless of who was considered attractive in high school.

TAKE A
Beauty Break

It's not easy to escape the beauty messages of the world we live in.

Too many of the businesses that support our entertainment media are all about turning your appearance insecurities into their profits. They know that the greater the difference between the good looks of the people they show you and your own, the more likely you are to run out to buy stuff.

Psychologists call this "discrepancy theory," and the formula is a proven one. But that doesn't mean it's inescapable. And the solution is refreshingly inexpensive. When what feels like the relentless onslaught of idealized perfection is getting you down, give yourself a beauty break: go offline, toss the fashion mag, turn off the TV, take a pass on the mall. Call a friend, listen to music, go outside.

The truth is, media junkies are more likely to worry about their appearance or suffer poor self-esteem than people who are too busy actually *doing* stuff to spend their time just watching TV or browsing online.

**"BEAUTIFUL YOUNG PEOPLE ARE ACCIDENTS OF NATURE, BUT BEAUTIFUL OLD PEOPLE ARE WORKS OF ART."
—FORMER FIRST LADY ELEANOR ROOSEVELT**

CHANGE THE
MESSAGE

◇◇◇◇◇◇◇◇◇◇◇◇◇◇◇◇◇◇◇

On the other hand, some forms of media can actually help you fight back against the beauty onslaught. Thanks to the internet, almost everyone has the tools to create their own, different messages, rather than merely absorbing images from big media companies and advertisers. And plenty of people are doing just that. If they feel excluded by the overwhelming thinness of bodies in mainstream fashion magazines, for example, they'll create blogs celebrating fuller-figured fashion. If they think an ad is objectifying, they'll post a critique on the company's social media page, or create a parody ad of their own. If they don't like the values promoted by media aimed at teens, they'll start their own web communities where girls have more to aspire to than losing five pounds or finding the perfect lip gloss.

Most of these efforts won't have the reach of a giant cosmetics campaign or hit TV show, of course. But there are more and more alternatives, if you look for them. And if you don't like the messages that magazines, blogs, ads, or TV shows are sending, or the beauty ideals they're promoting, it's good to speak up. If enough people complain—and stop buying, clicking, or watching—companies are eventually forced to listen and respond.

DOUBLE
Take

Think about the people around you whose company you genuinely enjoy. What do you like about them? Is it their perfect hair or toned abs? Or is it that they're easy to talk to, make you laugh, or have a talent you admire?

It would be wishful thinking to say that appearances don't matter—clearly they do. But not as much as we often imagine. And all the evidence suggests that other factors are much more important to leading a rewarding life. So, some final reflections:

The stress of keeping up appearances probably weighs heavier on people whose relationships—professional or personal—are more dependent on appearance in the first place.

People who aren't externally beautiful—even people whose appearances might at first be shocking—often develop inner personality resources that more than compensate. What some might see as a liability can be the very thing that helps those people stand out and make a difference in others' lives.

Remember: you have more media options, more ability to respond, and more tools to make your *own* media than any generation before you. You don't have to just sit back and watch while someone else tries to sell you a narrow idea of what beauty means.

What looks incredibly glamorous from the outside can be unfulfilling or very difficult from the inside.

Tuum Est

◇◇◇◇◇◇◇◇◇◇◇◇◇◇◇◇◇◇

... is a Latin phrase meaning "It's up to you."

Long before Nike turned "Just Do It" into an exercise mantra, or "go for it" became a common expression of encouragement, *tuum est* embodied the notion of free choice, underlining the fact that you get to decide: what you think about, who you admire, how you use your time, where you spend your money, what you do with the assets you've got. And which messages you buy in to about what's beautiful.

And the most important decision of all might be: do you invest energy in being critical of yourself and other people, or do you find ways to break free of media ideals instead?

The choice is yours. And every day, in dozens of small ways, you get to choose—you can wear makeup or go natural. Learn guitar or watch TV. Stare in the mirror or go for a run. Read a book or scan your Facebook feed. Fret over your flaws or not.

Some choices are more likely to make you feel good about who you are and what you can do in the world. To help you focus on *being*, instead of just *appearing* to be.

Tuum est.

NOTES

Introduction

Egyptian tomb. Cathy Newman, "The Enigma of Beauty," *National Geographic* online, Jan. 2000, science. nationalgeographic.com/science/health-and-human-body/human-body/enigma-beauty.

Chapter 1: Once Upon a Time

Disney Princesses. Peggy Orenstein, *Cinderella Ate My Daughter* (New York: HarperCollins, 2011), 19–32; Jenna Goudreau, "Disney Princess Tops List of the 20 Best-Selling Entertainment Products," *Forbes* online, Sept. 17, 2012, forbes.com/sites/jennagoudreau/2012/09/17/disney-princess-tops-list-of-the-20-best-selling-entertainment-products.

The Paper Bag Princess. Robert N. Munsch, *The Paper Bag Princess* (Toronto: Annick Press, 1980).

Greek gods and goddesses. Robert E. Bell, *Women of Classical Mythology: A Biographical Dictionary* (New York: Oxford University Press, 1991), 53–56; *Mythologica: A Treasury of World Myths and Legends* (Vancouver: Raincoast Books, 2003), 56–75.

Chapter 2: The Eye of the Beholder

measuring beauty. L.G. Farkas and I.R. Munro, eds., "The Validity of Neoclassical Facial Proportion Canons," *Anthropometric Facial Proportions in Medicine* (Springfield, IL: Charles C. Thomas, 1987), 57–66.

Peter Paul Rubens. *Theory of the Human Figure*, 1620, as cited in Arthur Marwick, *Beauty in History* (London: Thames and Hudson, 1988), 444.

Anna Utopia Giordano. Nick Squires, "The Size-Zero Botticellis," *Telegraph*, Feb. 10, 2012, telegraph.co.uk/news/worldnews/europe/italy/9074356/Size-zero-Botticellis-Anna-Utopia-Giordano-Photoshops-Venus-Renaissance-masterpieces-by-Titian.html.

hair. Nancy Etcoff, *Survival of the Prettiest: The Science of Beauty* (New York: Doubleday, 1999), 121–27.

average weight of fashion models. "Media Influence," Rader Programs, raderprograms.com/causes-statistics/media-eating-disorders.html.

changing body ideals. Joan Jacobs Brumberg, *The Body Project: An Intimate History of American Girls* (New York: Random House, 1997), 99–109; Kate Mulvey and Melissa Richards, *Decades of Beauty: The Changing Image of Women 1890s–1990s* (New York: Hamlyn, Octopus Publishing Group, 1998), 16–200; Roberta Pollack Seid, *Never Too Thin: Why Women Are at War with Their Bodies* (New York: Prentice Hall, 1989), 72–81; Terry Poulton, *No Fat Chicks: How Women Are Brainwashed To Hate Their Bodies and Spend Their Money* (Toronto: Key Porter, 1996), 48.

body image goes global. Lindy Sholes, "Society's Body Image: Perfect or Warped? Cultures View 'Ideal Beauty' Differently," *The Student Printz* (*University of Southern Mississippi*), July 18, 2003 (reporting on perspectives voiced in a panel discussion); Newman, "The Enigma of Beauty"; Julian Robinson, *The Quest for Human Beauty: An Illustrated History* (New York: W.W. Norton, 1998), 37, 85; Abigail Haworth, "Forced To Be Fat," *Marie Claire* online, July 21, 2011, marieclaire.com/world-reports/news/forcefeeding-in-mauritania.

Fiji eating disorders. Newman, "The Enigma of Beauty"; Erica Goode, "Study Finds TV Alters Fiji Girls' View of Body," *New York Times* online, May 20, 1999, nytimes.com/1999/05/20/world/study-finds-tv-alters-fiji-girls-view-of-body.html?src=pm.

81-year-old model. Piper Weiss, "Carmen Dell'Orefice, 81, Is Fashion Week's Oldest Runway Model. She's Also the Best," Yahoo! Shine, Sept. 10, 2012, shine.yahoo.com/the-thread-style-crush-carmen-dellorefice-81-fashion-weeks-oldest-runway-model-220400722.html.

amputee models. *The Debenhams Blog*, "Debenhams Shows Diversity in Fashion," April 11, 2013, blog.debenhams.com/debenhams-shows-diversity-in-fashion/fashion.

Chapter 3: The Young and the Healthy

anti-aging products. "Antiaging Products and Services: The Global Market," PR Newswire, Aug. 19, 2013, prnewswire.com/news-releases/antiaging-products-and-services-the-global-market-220249801.html.

blond hair. Doug Dollemore, "Gentlemen Prefer—Brunettes?" *Prevention* online, Dec. 2011, prevention.com/sex/sex-relationships/science-behind-attraction; "Sorry Marilyn, Gentlemen Don't Prefer Blondes," Badoo.com press release, Aug. 22, 2011, corp.badoo.com/cs/entry/press/33.

young models. Libby Copeland, "Tweens on the Runway," *Slate*, May 21, 2012, slate.com/articles/double_x/doublex/2012/05/pre_teen_runway_models_tracking_the_trend_.html.

psychologist quote. Newman, "The Enigma of Beauty."

evolution, natural selection. Helen E. Fisher, *The Sex Contract: The Evolution of Human Behavior* (New York: William Morrow, 1982), 87–123; Bertjan Doosje, "Partner Preferences as a Function of Gender, Age, Political Orientation and Level of Education," *Sex Roles: A Journal of Research* 40 (1–2): 45–60 (Jan. 1999); *The Nature of Sex: Sex and the Human Animal*, PBS Nature Series (video), 1992.

light skin. Etcoff, *Survival of the Prettiest*, 105.

scarring. Robinson, *The Quest for Human Beauty*, 85.

average. J.H. Langlois and L.A. Roggman, "Attractive Faces Are Only Average," *Psychological Science* I: 115–21 (1990); J.H. Koeslag, "Koinophilia Groups Sexual Creatures into Species, Promotes Stasis, and Stabilizes Social Behavior," *Journal of Theoretical Biology* 144: 15–35 (1990); "Measuring Beauty in Women," University of California Newsroom website, Dec. 16, 2009, universityofcalifornia.edu/news/article/22561; Face Research website, faceresearch.org.

new criteria. "Rethinking What We Want in a Partner," Northwestern University, Feb. 13, 2008, northwestern.edu/newscenter/stories/2008/02/partners.html; Eric Jaffe, "What Do Men Really Want?" *Psychology Today* online, March 13, 2012, psychologytoday.com/articles/201203/what-do-men-really-want; Sharon Jayson, "What Singles Want: Survey Looks at Attraction, Turnoffs," *USA Today* online, Feb. 5, 2013, usatoday.com/story/news/nation/2013/02/04/singles-dating-attraction-facebook/1878265.

Chapter 4: Suffering Is Optional

nail polish. Vicki Vantoch, "Fingernail Fashion Choices," *Washington Post* online, Dec. 28, 1999, washingtonpost.com/wp-srv/style/feed/a41653-1999dec28.htm.

tanning. "Tanning Salons in the U.S.: Market Research Report," IBISWorld, Aug. 2013, ibisworld.com/industry/default.aspx?indid=1721.

making up. Cathy Horyn, "At the Beauty Counter, It's Bait, Hook and Reel Them In," *New York Times*, Dec. 17, 2002; "What's Inside? That Counts: A Survey of Toxic Ingredients in Our Cosmetics," David Suzuki Foundation, Oct. 2010, davidsuzuki.org/publications/reports/2010/whats-inside-that-counts-a-survey-of-toxic-ingredients-in-our-cosmetics.

ancient makeup. Etcoff, *Survival of the Prettiest*, 101–3; Newman, "The Enigma of Beauty."

tattoos, scarification. Etcoff, *Survival of the Prettiest*, 99; Robinson, *The Quest for Human Beauty*, 81–83, 197; Judy Foreman, "Taking Health Risks for the Sake of Looks," *Boston Globe*, July 15, 2003.

tattoo removal. Natasha Singer, "Erasing Tattoos, Out of Regret or for a New Canvas," *New York Times* online, June 17, 2007, nytimes.com/2007/06/17/us/17tattoo.html?_r=1&.

Julia Roberts. "No-shave zone is sexy," *London Sunday Times*, May 30, 1999.

hair removal. Kirsten Hansen, "Hair or Bare? The History of American Women and Hair Removal, 1914–1934," Barnard College senior thesis, April 18, 2007, history.barnard.edu/sites/default/files/inline/kirstenhansen-thesis.pdf.

Balpreet Kaur. Lauren O'Neil, "Bearded Sikh Woman Teaches Reddit a Lesson," CBC online, Sept. 26, 2012, cbc.ca/newsblogs/yourcommunity/2012/09/bearded-sikh-woman-teaches-reddit-a-lesson.html.

foot-binding. San Francisco Museum, sfmuseum.org/chin/foot.html.

high heels. "High Heels: High Fashion That Can Hurt Your Feet," American Association of Women Podiatrists, aawpinc.com/news.htm; Gardiner Harris, "If Shoe Won't Fit, Fix the Foot? Popular Surgery Raises Concerns," *New York Times*, Dec. 7, 2003, A1; "Off with her pinky! How high heel–obsessed women are removing their toes with 'stiletto surgery' for a comfier fit," *Mail Online*, Nov. 20, 2012, dailymail.co.uk/femail/article-2236039/Off-pinky-How-high-heel-obsessed-women-removing-toes-stiletto-surgery-comfier-fit.html.

rib removal. A. Dillon-Malone, ed. *Women on Women and on Age, Beauty, Love, Men, Marriage* (London: MacMillan, 1995), 81; Barbara Mikkelson, "Getting Waisted," Snopes, July 8, 2006, snopes.com/horrors/vanities/ribs.asp.

plastic surgery history. Elizabeth Haiken, *Venus Envy: A History of Plastic Surgery* (Baltimore: Johns Hopkins University Press, 1997), 1–49; Sander L. Gilman, *Making the Body Beautiful: A Cultural History of Aesthetic Surgery* (Princeton: Princeton University Press, 1999), 3–118, 152–177.

plastic surgery statistics. "13.8 Million Cosmetic Plastic Surgery Procedures Performed in 2011," American Society of Plastic Surgeons website, Feb. 9, 2012, plasticsurgery.org/news-and-resources/press-release-archives/2012-press-release-archives/138-million-cosmetic-plastic-surgery-procedures-performed-in-2011.html.

breast implants. Leslie Kaufman, "And Now, a Few More Words about Breasts," *New York Times,* Sept. 17, 2000; Krista Foss and Montana Burnett, "The Promise of Perfection," *Globe and Mail*, June 21, 2001; Alissa Quart, *Branded: The Buying and Selling of Teenagers* (Cambridge: Perseus Publishing, 2003); Andrea Petersen, "Once Banned, Silicone Breast Implants Make a Comeback," *Wall Street Journal* online, March 11, 2013, online.wsj.com/news/articles/SB10001424127887324735 304578354112677417392; "Risks of Breast Implants," U.S. Food and Drug Administration website, retrieved June 16, 2013, from fda.gov/MedicalDevices/Products andMedicalProcedures/ImplantsandProsthetics /Breastimplants/ucm064106.htm.

butt augmentation. Lauren Cox, "Beauty Queen's Death Shows Dangers of Buttock Implants," ABC News online, Dec. 2, 2009, abcnews.go.com/Health/Cosmetic/miss-argentinas-death-shows-dangers-buttock-injections/story?id=9221615#.UZ6EoOAXilc.

anabolic steroids. Natalie Angier, "Drugs, Sports, Body Image and G.I. Joe," *New York Times* online, Dec. 22, 1998, nytimes.com/1998/12/22/science/drugs-sports-body-image-and-gi-joe.html.

Chapter 5: Double Standard

Drew Barrymore quote. Allison Glock, "Drew Barrymore Can Do No Wrong," *Elle*, Jan. 2004.

Helena Rubenstein quote. Mulvey and Richards, *Decades of Beauty*, 207.

male beauty, dandyism, industrial revolution. Robinson, *The Quest for Human Beauty*, 44, 193, 203.

male gaze. John Berger, *Ways of Seeing* (London: BBC/ Penguin Books, 1977), 46–47.

Alex Bilmes. Remarks to panel at Advertising Week Europe conference, March 19, 2013, as reported by *The Guardian*, guardian.co.uk/media/2013/mar/19/ esquire-editor-show-women-like-cars.

GI Joe. Natalie Angier, "Drugs, Sports, Body Image and G.I. Joe," *New York Times* online, Dec. 22, 1998, nytimes.com/1998/12/22/science/drugs-sports-body-image-and-gi-joe.html?pagewanted=all&src=pm.

video games and self-image. Christopher P. Barlett and Richard J. Harris, "The Impact of Body Emphasizing Video Games on Body Image Concerns in Men and Women," *Sex Roles* 59: 586–601 (2008), doi 10.1007/ s11199-008-9457-8.

American Apparel ads. Emelie Frida Eriksson, "American Apparel Really Know about That 'Unisex' Thing. Damn Well," *En Blommig Tekopp* (blog), May 14, 2013, enblommigtekopp.blogg.se/2013/may/ american-apparel-really-know-about-that-unisex-thing-damn-well-english-version.html.

reversing gender roles in ads. Sarah Zelinski, Kayla Hatzel, and Dylan Lambi-Raine, "Representations of Gender in Advertising" (video), April 3, 2013, youtube.com/watch v=HaB2b1w52yE&feature= youtu.be.

magazines and weight. Amy R. Malkin, "Women and Weight: Gendered Messages on Magazine Covers," *Sex Roles: A Journal of Research* 40 (7–8): 647–55 (April 1999); A.E. Andersen and L. DiDomenico, "Diet vs. Shape Content of Popular Male and Female Magazines: A Dose-Response Relationship to the Incidence of Eating Disorders?" *International Journal of Eating Disorders*, 11: 283–87 (1992), doi: 10.1002/1098-108X(199204)11:3<283::AID-EAT 2260110313>3.0.CO;2-O.

casting couch. Coeli Carr, "Tales from the Casting Couch: Hollywood's Ugly Open Secret," ABC News online, Oct. 12, 2010, abcnews.go.com/ entertainment/gwyneth-paltrow-lisa-rinna-sexual-politics-casting-couch/story?id=11849706#. UaURNeAXilc.

female actors' earning potential. Edward Guthmann, "Many Actresses Hitting Middle Age Find Themselves Desperate for Good Parts," *San Francisco Chronicle* online, Aug. 15, 2003, sfgate. com/entertainment/article/Many-actresses-hitting-middle-age-find-themselves-2596633.php.

men's beauty spending. Karyn Siegel-Maier, "Skincare is Just for Women, Right? Guess Again!" *Better Nutrition*, July 2001; "Men's Grooming Market Expected to Hit $84+ Billion by 2014," MarketResearch.com, Nov. 9, 2009, marketwired.com/press-release/ mens-grooming-market-expected-to-hit-84-billion-by-2014-1173523.htm.

Chapter 6: Beauty Power

ugly laws. Sander L. Gilman, *Making the Body Beautiful: A Cultural History of Aesthetic Surgery* (Princeton: Princeton University Press, 1999), 24.

Chanel Iman. Tim Teeman, "Chanel Iman: Modelling, Racism and Me," *The Times Magazine*, Feb. 16, 2013, thetimes.co.uk/tto/magazine/article3684885.ece.

Bess Myerson. Susan Dworkin, *Miss America, 1945: Bess Myerson's Own Story* (New York: Newmarket Press, 1999), 183, 196.

plastic surgery and ethnicity. "AAFPRS 2012 Statistics on Trends in Facial Plastic Surgery," American Academy of Facial Plastic and Reconstructive Surgery website, aafprs.org/media/stats_polls/m_stats.html.

nose jobs. Holly Brubach, "Beauty under the Knife," *Atlantic Monthly* online, Feb. 2000, theatlantic.com/ past/docs/issues/2000/02/002brubach.htm; Rita Rubin, "A Nose Dive for Nose Jobs," *Tablet*, June 7, 2012, tabletmag.com/jewish-life-and-religion/101732/a-nose-dive-for-nose-jobs.

eyelid surgery. Ioannis P. Glavas, "The ABC's of Asian Blepharoplasty or 'Double Eyelid' Surgery," Marketwired, Aug. 11, 2011, marketwired.com/ press-release/the-abcs-of-asian-blepharoplasty-or-double-eyelid-surgery-1548793.htm; Ann Oldenburg, "Julie Chen Had Plastic Surgery To Make Eyes 'Bigger,'" *USA Today*, Sept. 12, 2013, usatoday.com/story/life/ people/2013/09/12/julie-chen-plastic-eye-surgery-less-chinese/2803049.

skin lighteners, hair products. Kathy Peiss, *Hope in a Jar: The Making of America's Beauty Culture* (New York: Metropolitan Books, Henry Holt, 1998), 52.

skin lightening in India. Anjana Gosai, "India's Myth of Fair-Skinned Beauty," *The Guardian* online, July 19, 2010, theguardian.com/lifeandstyle/2010/jul/19/india-fair-skinned-beauty; Monisha Rajesh, "India's Unfair Obsession with Lighter Skin," *The Guardian* online, Aug. 14, 2013, theguardian.com/world/shortcuts/2013/ aug/14/indias-dark-obsession-fair-skin.

Solange Knowles. Kristie Lau, "Solange Knowles Proudly Defends Her Afro after Critics Call Her Natural Hair 'Unkempt' and 'Dry as Heck,'" *Mail Online*, June 12, 2012, dailymail.co.uk/femail/article-2158324/ Solange-Knowles-proudly-defends-afro-critics-natural-hair-unkempt-dry-heck.html.

size bias. R. Puhl and K.D. Brownell, "Bias, Discrimination, and Obesity," Rudd Center for Food Policy & Obesity, Yale University, yaleruddcenter.org/resources/ upload/docs/what/bias/WeightBias_Philadelphia DPH_3.11.pdf; "Facts on Size Discrimination," National Association to Advance Fat Acceptance, naafaonline. com/dev2/assets/documents/naafa_FactSheet_v17_ screen.pdf.

reality vs. tv. Bradley S. Greenberg et al. "Portrayals of Overweight and Obese Individuals on Commercial Television," *American Journal of Public Health* 93 (8): 1342–48 (Aug. 2003).

disordered eating. Health Communication Research Laboratory, hcrl.slu.edu/HCRL/Programs/TeentoTeen/Eatingdisorders/effects.html; Mirasol Recovery Centers, "Eating Disorder Statistics," mirasol.net/eating-disorders/information/eating-disorder-statistics.php.

weight and health. Gina Kolata, "Chubby Gets a Second Look," *New York Times* online, Nov. 11, 2007, nytimes.com/2007/11/11/weekinreview/11kolata.html?_r=1&; Sora Song, "Fat Stigma: How Online News May Worsen the Problem of Obesity," *Time* online, May 12, 2011, healthland.time.com/2011/05/12/fat-stigma-how-online-news-worsens-the-problem-of-obesity.

vanity sizing. Stephanie Clifford, "One Size Fits Nobody," *New York Times* online, April 25, 2011, nytimes.com/2011/04/25/business/25sizing.html?_r=0.

jeans. Eric Noll, "Denim Dilemma: Does Getting a Lot Mean Paying a Lot?" ABC News online, April 24, 2010, abcnews.go.com/GMA/Weekend/cheap-jeans-expensive-jeans-difference/story?id=10462455#.UbeD3uBe-aA; "How Can Jeans Cost $300?" *The Wall Street Journal* online, July 7, 2011, online.wsj.com/news/articles/SB10001424052702303365804576429730284498872.

cool hunt. Malcolm Gladwell, "The Coolhunt," *The New Yorker* online, March 17, 1997, newyorker.com/archive/1997/03/17/1997_03_17_078_TNY_CARDS_000378002.

tattoos and clothing laws. Etcoff, *Survival of the Prettiest*, 218–19; Robinson, *The Quest for Human Beauty*, 83.

Chapter 7: Opportunity or Knocks?

guilty. R. Mazzella and A. Feingold, "The Effects of Physical Attractiveness, Race, Socioeconomic Status, and Gender of Defendants and Victims on Judgments of Mock Jurors: A Meta-Analysis," *Journal of Applied Social Psychology* 24: 1315–44 (1994); George Lowery, "Study Uncovers Why Jurors Reward the Good-looking, Penalize the Unbeautiful," *Cornell Chronicle*, May 11, 2010, news.cornell.edu/stories/2010/05/unattractive-people-pay-price-court.

flat tire. R. Athanasiou and P. Greene, "Physical Attractiveness and Helping Behavior," *Proceedings of the 81st Annual Convention of the American Psychological Association* 8: 289–90 (1973), as cited by Etcoff, *Survival of the Prettiest*, 45.

Gabourey Sidibe quote. Laura Brown, "Being Precious: Gabourey Sidibe," *Harper's Bazaar* online, Jan. 7, 2010, harpersbazaar.com/fashion/fashion-articles/gabourey-sidibe-precious-interview-0210.

more confidence. Alan Feingold, "Good-looking People Are Not What We Think," *Psychological Bulletin* 111: 304–41 (1992).

control of lives. R. Anderson, "Physical Attractiveness and Locus of Control," *Journal of Social Psychology* 105: 213–16 (1978).

more assertive. D.J. Jackson and T.L. Huston, "Physical Attractiveness and Assertiveness," *Journal of Social Psychology* 96: 79–84 (1975).

beauty in the workplace. Daniel S. Hamermesh and Jeff E. Biddle, "Beauty and the Labor Market," National Bureau of Economic Research, Nov. 1993; "The Right To Be Beautiful," *Economist* 367 (May 24, 2003): 9; Markus M. Mobius and Tanya S. Rosenblat, "Why Beauty Matters," Harvard University's DASH repository, June 24, 2005, nrs.harvard.edu/urn-3:HUL.InstRepos:3043406; Timothy A. Judge, Charlice Hurst, and Lauren S. Simon, "Does It Pay To Be Smart, Attractive, or Confident (or All Three)? Relationships among General Mental Ability, Physical Attractiveness, Core Self-Evaluations, and Income," *Journal of Applied Psychology* 94 (3): 742–755 (2009); Stefanie K. Johnson et al., "Physical Attractiveness Biases in Ratings of Employment Suitability: Tracking Down the "Beauty Is Beastly" Effect," *The Journal of Social Psychology*, 150 (3): 301–18 (2010); Maria Agthea, Matthias Spörrlea, and Jon K. Manerb, "Don't Hate Me Because I'm Beautiful: Anti-attractiveness Bias in Organizational Evaluation and Decision Making," *Journal of Experimental Social Psychology*, 46 (6): 1151–54 (Nov. 2010).

beauty in school. Philip Kenneth Robins et al. "Effects of Physical Attractiveness, Personality, and Grooming on Academic Performance in High School," *Labour Economics* 16 (4): 373–82 (Aug. 2009).

cute babies. Rinah Yamamoto et al., "Gender Differences in the Motivational Processing of Babies Are Determined by Their Facial Attractiveness," *PLoS ONE* 4 (6): e6042 (June 24, 2009), doi:10.1371/journal.pone.0006042.

women and men on the phone. M. Snyder, E.D. Tanke, and E. Berscheid, "Social Perception and Interpersonal Behavior: On the Self-fulfilling Nature of Social Stereotypes," *Journal of Personality and Social Psychology* 24: 285–90 (1972).

height matters. P. Douglas Filaroski, "Tall People Get Perks on the Job," *Jacksonville Business Journal*, Oct. 17, 2003, bizjournals.com/jacksonville/stories/2003/10/13/daily34.html.

bottom line on beauty advantages. Etcoff, *Survival of the Prettiest*, 50.

beauty and integrity. A.H. Eagly, R.D. Ashmore, M.G. Makhijani, and L.C. Longo, "What Is Beautiful Is Good, But...: A Meta-Analytic Review of Research on the Physical Attractiveness Stereotype," *Psychological Bulletin* 110: 109–28 (1991).

being asked to help. A. Naadler, R. Phapira, and S. Ben-Itzhak, "Good Looks May Help: Effects of Helper's Physical Attractiveness and Sex of Helper on Males' and Females' Help-seeking Behavior," *Journal of Personality and Social Psychology* 42: 90–99 (1982).

Joan Collins. Dillon-Malone, *Women on Women*, 85.

unearned advantage. Elizabeth Nickson, "Ruminations on Age and Beauty," *Globe and Mail*, May 26, 1999.

Pantene ad. Nancy Friday, *The Power of Beauty* (New York: Harper Collins, 1996), 78.

contrast effect. D.T. Kenrick and S.E. Gutierres, "Contrast Effects and Judgments of Physical Attractiveness: When Beauty Becomes a Social Problem," *Journal of Personality and Social Psychology* 38: 131–40 (1980).

beautiful women not promoted. T.F. Cash and R.N. Kilcullen, "The Eye of the Beholder: Susceptibility to Sexism and Beautyism in the Evaluation of Managerial Applicants," *Journal of Applied Social Psychology* 15: 591–605 (1985).

fired banker. Elizabeth Dwoskin, "Is This Woman Too Hot To Be a Banker?" *The Village Voice*, June 1, 2010, villagevoice.com/2010-06-01/news/is-this-woman-too-hot-to-work-in-a-bank.

Candice Bergen. Elaine Dutka, "Candice Bergen: One Cool, Classy Cookie," *Cosmopolitan*, Oct. 1993, 182.

Clara Bow. Paul Donnelley, *Fade to Black: A Book of Movie Obituaries* (London: Omnibus Press, 2000), 114.

Chapter 8: Competition 24/7

P.T. Barnum, history of Miss America pageant. "Miss America," Public Broadcasting Service, pbs.org/wgbh/amex/missamerica/index.html; Candace Savage, *Beauty Queens: A Playful History* (Vancouver: Greystone Books/Douglas and McIntyre, 1998), 15–55.

brown paper bag contest. Elizabeth Haiken, *Venus Envy: A History of Cosmetic Surgery* (Baltimore: Johns Hopkins University Press, 1997), 12.

pageant pros and cons. Jill Filipovic, "The Miss USA Pageant: How Far We Haven't Come," *The Huffington Post*, March 23, 2007, huffingtonpost.com/jill-filipovic/the-miss-usa-pageant-how-_b_44130.html.

child beauty pageants. Kristen Schultz and Ann Pleshette Murphy, "Beauty Pageants Draw Children and Criticism," ABC News online, Feb. 26, 2013, abcnews.go.com/GMA/story?id=126315&page=1#.UdMFSOBe-aA.

Mallory Hytes Hagan. Josh Grossberg, "Miss America Mallory Hytes Hagan Reacts to Tabloid Criticisms About Her Putting on Weight," E! Online, March 15, 2013, ca.eonline.com/news/398057/miss-america-mallory-hytes-hagan-reacts-to-tabloid-criticisms-about-her-putting-on-weight.

1968 protest. Susan J. Douglas, *Where the Girls Are: Growing up Female with the Mass Media* (New York: Times Books, 1994), 139–41.

media effects. Heidi D. Posavac, "Exposure to Media Images of Female Attractiveness and Concern with Body Weight among Young Women," *Sex Roles: A Journal of Research* 38 (3–4): 187–201 (Feb. 1998).

impact of photography. Peiss, *Hope in a Jar*, 45.

internet and self-image. M. Tiggemann and A. Slater, "NetGirls: The Internet, Facebook, and Body Image Concern in Adolescent Girls," *The International Journal of Eating Disorders* 46 (6): 630–3 (Sept. 2013), doi: 10.1002/eat.22141.

Facebook. Stephanie Hanes, "Facebook May Amplify Eating Disorders and Poor Body Image," *The Christian Science Monitor* online, March 30, 2012, csmonitor.com/The-Culture/Family/2012/0330/Facebook-may-amplify-eating-disorders-and-poor-body-image.

Lights! Cameras! Botox! Aaron Sands, "High-Definition TV Exposes Hollywood's Ugly Truths," *Ottawa Citizen*, May 30, 2003.

Photoshop. "5 Celebrities Rejecting Hollywood's Photoshop Fever," DoSomething.org, dosomething.org/news/5-celebrities-rejecting-hollywoods-photoshop-fever.

Julia Bluhm. Dodai Stewart, "Girls ask *Teen Vogue* to Ditch Photoshop, Get Berated by Editor-in-Chief," *Jezebel*, July 12, 2012, jezebel.com/5925420/girls-ask-teen-vogue-to-ditch-photoshop-get-berated-by-editor+in+chief.

Coco Rocha. "She has the name of a fashion icon, the spirit of a maverick," *The Gazette* (Montreal), April 30, 2008, canada.com/topics/lifestyle/style/story.html?id=22038051-bcca-4e05-8918-a4f53a17cfa9.

Barbie. "Dying To Be Barbie," Rehabs.com, rehabs.com/explore/dying-to-be-barbie/#.UvvJeyhbmaA.

average height and weight. C.D. Fryar, Q. Gu, C.L. Ogden, "Anthropometric Reference Data for Children and Adults: United States, 2007–2010," National Center for Health Statistics, *Vital and Health Statistics* 11 (252), Oct. 2012.

Bobbi Brown. Bobbi Brown, Anne Marie Iverson, *Bobbi Brown Teenage Beauty: Everything You Need to Look Pretty, Natural, Sexy and Awesome* (New York: Harper Collins, 2000), 143.

model behavior. Kirstie Clements, *The Vogue Factor* (London: Guardian Faber, 2013).

Chapter 9: Flogging Fantasies

prohibition against makeup. Savage, *Beauty Queens*, 41.

beauty by the numbers. "Beauty Industry 2012 Outlook," Demeter Group, demetergroup.net/docs/whitepapers/Demeter_Group_Beauty_Industry_2012_Outlook.pdf; "Weight Loss Market in U.S. Up 1.7% to $61 Billion," PRWeb, April 16, 2013, prweb.com/releases/2013/4/prweb10629316.htm; "Cosmetic Procedures Increase in 2012," American Society for Aesthetic Plastic Surgery Press Center, March 12, 2013, surgery.org/media/news-releases/cosmetic-procedures-increase-in-2012; "Up to the Minute, Kidman's a Real Earner," *The Sydney Morning Herald* online, Sept. 29, 2006, smh.com.au/articles/2006/09/29/1159337326786.html; "TBC Beauty Facts, Figures, and Trends," The Beauty

Company, June 2012, thebeautycompany.co/downloads/Beyer_BeautyNumbers.pdf; Barbara Thau, "Behind the Spritz: What Really Goes Into a Bottle of $100 Perfume," DailyFinance, May 22, 2012, dailyfinance.com/2012/05/22/celebrity-perfume-cost-breakdown.

L'Oréal. Amy Verner, "L'Oréal's 'Because I'm worth it' slogan marks a milestone," *The Globe and Mail* online, Dec. 2, 2011, theglobeandmail.com/life/fashion-and-beauty/beauty/loreals-because-im-worth-it-slogan-marks-a-milestone/article554604.

deceptive advertising. Paula Begoun, *Blue Eyeshadow Should Absolutely Be Illegal: The Definitive Guide to Skin Care and Makeup Application* (Seattle: Beginning Press, 1994), 12–21; Hillary Chura, "On Cosmetics: Marketing Rules All," *New York Times* online, Nov. 18, 2006, nytimes.com/2006/11/18/business/18instincts.html?_r=1&; Louise Hall, "Warning over Cosmetics Claims," *The Sydney Morning Herald* online, May 11, 2009, smh.com.au/lifestyle/beauty/warning-over-cosmetics-claims-20090510-az7g.html; The Beauty Brains website, thebeautybrains.com; "On Myths and Makeup" (podcast), Token Skeptic website, April 24, 2012, tokenskeptic.org/2012/04/24/episode-one-hundred-and-fifteen-on-myths-and-makeup-pseudoscience-and-cosmetics; Ben Goldacre, "Attack of the Wrinkled Ladies," *The Guardian*, May 5, 2007, badscience.net/2007/05/410.

mascara ads. Charlotte Cowles, "Maybelline and Lancôme Ads Banned in the U.K. for Excessive Airbrushing," *TheCut* (blog), NYMag.com, July 27, 2011, nymag.com/thecut/2011/07/julia-roberts-ad-banned.html; Lindsey Hunter Lopez, "Taylor Swift's CoverGirl ad pulled," *The Marquee Blog,* CNN Entertainment, Dec. 21, 2011, marquee.blogs.cnn.com/2011/12/21/taylor-swifts-covergirl-ad-pulled.

price of cosmetics. Anneli Rufus, "The Cosmetics Racket," *AlterNet*, Sept. 10, 2010, alternet.org/story/148140/the_cosmetics_racket%3A_why_the_beauty_industry_can_get_away_with_charging_a_fortune_for_makeup.

lingerie advertising. Bernadette Morra, "La Senza's Better Way to Grab Our Attention," *Toronto Star*, Dec. 4, 2003.

credibility on a diet. James Cummings, "Putting the Squeeze on Diet Scams: Truth vs Fiction," *New York Times*, Feb. 5, 2003; ABC News Staff, "100 Million Dieters, $20 Billion: The Weight-Loss Industry by the Numbers," ABC News online, May 8, 2012, abcnews.go.com/Health/100-million-dieters-20-billion-weight-loss-industry/story?id=16297197; T. Mann et al., "Medicare's Search for Effective Obesity Treatments: Diets Are Not the Answer," *American Psychologist*, 62 (3): 220–33 (Apr. 2007); Melanie Haiken, "5 Deadliest Diet Trends: Pills That Really Can Kill," *Forbes* online, April 19, 2012, forbes.com/sites/melaniehaiken/2012/04/19/5-deadliest-diet-trends.

Don't Smile for the Camera. Laura M. Holson, "A Little Too Ready for Her Close-Up?" *New York Times* online, April 23, 2010, nytimes.com/2010/04/25/fashion/25natural.html?pagewanted=all&_r=0.

makeovers. Ruth Shalit, "Extreme Makeover: The Truth Behind the TV Show," *Elle*, Jan. 2004; Jill Smolowe and Mike Neill, "Total Makeover," *People* online, Nov. 17, 2003, people.com/people/archive/article/0,,20148631,00.html.

Clinton Kelly. Chris Harnick, "'What Not To Wear' Canceled: TLC Series Ending After 10 Years," *The Huffington Post*, March 6, 2013, huffingtonpost.com/2013/03/06/what-not-to-wear-canceled-tlc-series-ending_n_2819896.html.

Heidi Montag. "*The Hills*: Heidi's Mom Reacts to Plastic Surgeries," *People* online, April 28, 2010, people.com/people/article/0,,20421071,00.html.

Chapter 10: Beyond Image

looks and happiness. Daniel S. Hamermesh, *Beauty Pays: Why Attractive People Are More Successful* (Princeton: Princeton University Press, 2011), 174.

James Partridge. Elizabeth Austin, "Marks of Mystery," *Psychology Today* online, July 1999, psychologytoday.com/articles/199907/marks-mystery.

Agata. Interview by author for TV series *DoubleTake*, broadcast on WTN, 1996. Elia Saikaly. Personal interview with author, Oct. 15, 2003.

teenage girls in UK. Mark Gould, "Girls Choosing Camera Lenses over Microscopes," *The Guardian* online, Oct. 3, 2008, theguardian.com/education/2008/oct/03/science.choosingadegree.

realities of modeling. The Model Alliance survey, modelalliance.org/industry-analysis; Ashley Stetts, "Real Talk: How Much Models Actually Get Paid," *XOJane*, Sept. 24, 2012, xojane.com/issues/real-talk-how-much-models-actually-get-paid; "Sara Ziff's Picture Me Documentary Uncovers Sexual Assault in the Modeling World," Popsugar, June 8, 2009, fashionologie.com/sara-ziff-picture-me-documentary-uncovers-sexual-assault-modeling-world-3271323.

Coco Rocha. "CFDA Panel on Skinny Models: Coco Rocha on Her Struggle," *TheCut* (blog), NYMag.com, June 11, 2008, nymag.com/thecut/2008/06/cfdas_takes_on_the_tooskinny_m_1.html.

personality research. Clyde Haberman, "The Essence of Beauty? Ooh La Loren," *New York Times*, May 9, 2001; Nicole Bode, "Put on a Happy Face," *Psychology Today* online, Jan. 2001, psychologytoday.com/articles/200101/put-happy-face.

discrepancy theory. Nicholas Lezard, "You Really Can't Take it With You," *Guardian Weekly*, Oct. 30, 2003, 19.

ACKNOWLEDGMENTS

The author would like to thank:

Paula Ayer for her resourcefulness, insight, and sensitivity in finding new research and examples, and carefully integrating them, editing and adapting other sections to better fit the new, more graphic design, and effectively matching the tone and style of my original text;

Natalie Olsen for enlivening the book with a design and visual elements that significantly enhance the text;

Karen Klassen and Katy Lemay for their creative illustrations that effectively illuminate the book's themes;

Morgan Reynolds, Elia Saikaly, Rosanna Majeed, Val Brousseau, Amanda Parriag, and Agata Kesik for overcoming the embarrassment implicit in the act of giving an interview about growing up beautiful;

Tom, Lev, Brook, Nathan, and Tim for giving up a Sunday afternoon to talk about beauty;

Megan and Elizabeth for sharing their personal experiences and perceptions;

Renate Mohr for being a wonderfully supportive and perceptive first reader;

Alexandra Boothroyd for her thoughtful comments on the revised text;

Pam Robertson, whose unerring instincts provided crucial direction for the book's shape and tone;

my parents, Norma and West, for raising me to care more about substance than image;

and most of all,

David Mitchell, whose expressed love and appreciation provide invaluable support for my ongoing efforts to practice what I preach.

IMAGE CREDITS

INDEX

ABOUT THE AUTHOR AND ILLUSTRATORS

Shari Graydon, the award-winning author of *Made You Look: How Advertising Works and Why You Should Know*, has written columns for newspapers, commentaries for radio, speeches for politicians, chapters for textbooks, and programs for television. She has taught media literacy at university and is a former president of the nonprofit women's group Media Action, all of which helped her to write this book.

Shari now lives in Ottawa, Ontario, where she runs a social enterprise called Informed Opinions. She trains smart women and girls to speak up more often, and delivers keynote presentations called "In Search of More Fully-Clothed Female Role Models."

Karen Klassen's illustrations have appeared in advertising campaigns and magazines as well as on beer cans and snowboards. She works in a variety of mediums including screenprinting, watercolor, acrylic, and oils. Her illustrations have won awards from The Society of Illustrators of Los Angeles, *Communication Arts*, *American Illustration*, and The Black Book AR100, to name a few. She occasionally teaches at the Alberta College of Art and Design and has clients all over Canada, the United States, and Europe.

Katy Lemay developed an overwhelming passion for illustration while completing her Bachelor of Graphic Design at the University of Quebec in Montreal. During that time she created her unique style of collage combining objects and photographs, which enables her to create one-of-a-kind images. Katy's many clients include *Time*, *The Globe and Mail*, *The Boston Globe*, *Azure*, and *L'Actualité*.